Editorial Project Manager:
Elizabeth Morris, Ph. D.

Editor in Chief:
Sharon Coan, M.S. Ed.

Art Director:
Elayne Roberts

Art Coordinator Assistant:
Cheri Macoubrie Wilson

Production Manager:
Phil Garcia

Imaging:
Ralph Olmedo, Jr.

Publishers:
Rachelle Cracchiolo, M.S. Ed.
Mary Dupuy Smith, M.S. Ed.

Internet Resources for Educators

Author:

Timothy Hopkins

Teacher Created Materials, Inc.
6421 Industry Way
Westminster, CA 92683
ISBN-1-57690-458-X

©1999 Teacher Created Materials, Inc.
Made in U.S.A.

Teacher Created Materials

Table of Contents

Art

Art Exploration: A Global Approach

http://www.artsednet.getty.edu/ArtsEdNet/Resources/Sampler/f.html

---

The Getty Center for Education in the Arts created this high school unit to be used as part of an introductory art course or as a course to meet graduation requirements in art, which an increasing number of states mandate. Categories: Ceramics, Painting, Sculpture

Notes:

_____

_____

_____

_____

Art for Kids

http://artforkids.tqn.com/library/weekly/aa092497.htm

Color pictures right on the Web! This is just one of the cool features at this very appealing site. Also features reviewed art links (in categories) and coloring contests.

Notes:

_____

_____

_____

_____

Art Lesson Plans

http://www.bway.net/~starlite/projects.htm

Included are lesson plans on stained glass, primary colors, murals, mobiles, and collages, which come with grade recommendations, materials lists, and procedures.

Notes:

_____

_____

_____

_____

@rt Room

http://www.arts.ufl.edu/art/rt_room/@rtroom_home.html

This helpful site features interactive art activities and includes demonstrations and tips on how to think like an artist. There's a section for teachers (art sparkers) that features activities to do in the classroom.

Notes:

_____

_____

_____

_____

Art Teacher Connection

http://www.primenet.com/~arted/

Bettie Lake, an art teacher from Phoenix, dedicates this site to encouraging innovation in art education through new technologies. Features include links to lesson plans, opportunities to contact other teachers interested in art, and links to reviewed art sites.

Notes:

_____

_____

_____

_____

Art Teacher on the Net

http://members.tripod.com/~artworkinparis/index-3.html

Included in art ideas for teachers, parents, and kids are features of teacher-submitted art ideas, a free art project of the week, and art lessons from all over the world.

Notes:

_____

_____

_____

_____

Arts Education and School Improvement Resources for Local and State Leaders

http://www.ed.gov/pubs/ArtsEd/

Find here a guide for local and state leaders on how to improve art education, secure funding from the U.S. Department of Education for improving arts education, and use the arts to improve overall student performance.

Notes:

_____

_____

_____

ArtsEdge Network

http://artsedge.kennedy-center.org/artsedge.html

The Curriculum Studio portion of this excellent site from the Kennedy Center for the Performing Arts is designed to guide teachers seeking innovative instructional strategies and resources to enhance or expand existing curricula and/or to create curricula that address new standards for the arts and other subject areas.
Categories: News, Spotlight, Curriculum Studio, For Students

Notes:

_____

_____

_____

ArtsEdNet

http://www.artsednet.getty.edu/

This art site from the Getty Institute for the Arts features lesson plans and curriculum ideas, image galleries (somewhat limited), and links to other WWW art sites.

Notes:

_____

_____

_____

_____

Crayola Art Education

http://education.crayola.com/

The main concentration of this site is to market Crayola's products, but it is worth a visit for the Art Techniques section, which offers tips on using many different kinds of applications. Categories: Art Techniques, Dream-Makers, Model Magic Activities, Educational Products, Talk About Art (discussion group)

Notes:

_____

_____

_____

_____

CyberKids Home

http://www.cyberkids.com

A site designed for younger kids to publish their artwork, writing, and even music (in midi format only), this is a very highly-awarded site, one of the first and still one of the best. Categories: Contests, Gallery, Games and Puzzles, Reading Room, Young Composers

Notes:

_____

_____

_____

_____

Eyes on Art

http://www.kn.pacbell.com/wired/art/art.html

A great site for students and teachers that explores many different aspects of art, it also has interactive lessons and tips on how to use them. Categories: Visual Glossary, Artistic Styles, 2 View 4 U, Teacher's Guide, Links, Quiz

Notes:

_____

_____

_____

_____

Favorite Lessons

http://www.artswire.org/kenroar/lessons/lessons.html

Part of the Incredible Art Department's site, this page features over 100 art lessons submitted by teachers and covers pre-primary to undergraduate students. Many of the lessons are very detailed and very well-crafted. Categories: Early Childhood, Elementary, Elementary Drama and Art, Jr. High/Middle School, High School, Undergraduate

Notes:

_____

_____

_____

From Windmills to Whirligigs

http://www.sci.mus.mn.us/sln/vollis

The Whirligig Farm is an in-depth exploration of science and art, concentrating on whirligigs, windmills and kinetic sculpture. It is lots of fun, created by the Science Museum of Minnesota and their partner school, Museum Magnet School in St. Paul, MN. Categories: Tour, Activities

Notes:

_____

_____

_____

Global Show-n-Tell Home Page

http://www.telenaut.com/gst/

Literacy isn't just reading and writing. Artwork, too, is a method of displaying your knowledge and appreciating the insights of others. This page lets children show their work to kids around the world and has lots of links to children's art works on the Web.

Notes:

_____

_____

_____

_____

Imagination Factory

http://users.hsonline.net/kidatart/

An excellent site devoted to recycling, the *Imagination Factory* includes lessons, activities, and links to other art and environmental sites on the Web. Categories: Creative, Education, Lessons/Activities, Links

Notes:

_____

_____

_____

_____

Incredible Art Department

http://www.artswire.org/kenroar/

From art news to hundreds of lesson plans, this site is a cornucopia of art resources on the Web. It contains links to over a thousand other art sites on the Web and free software downloads (mostly for Macs). Categories: Art Room, Lessons, Art Jobs, Art News

Notes:

_____

_____

_____

_____

Michael C. Carlos Museum

http://www.cc.emory.edu/CARLOS/carlos.html

At this site are art collections from Ancient Egypt, the Ancient Near East, the Sub-Sahara, and an impressive collection of art from the Ancient Americas. Other Categories: History of the Museum, Classical Art, Works of Art on Paper

Notes:

_____

_____

_____

_____

Musée du Louvre

http://www.paris.org./Musees/Louvre/

This impressive resource contains most of the famous paintings housed in the Louvre, the museum's floor plan, and a short history of the museum.

Notes:

_____

_____

_____

_____

National Arts and Humanities Education Program

http://nmaa-ryder.si.edu/deptdir/edusub/nahep.html

The Educational Research Department of the NMAA creates education materials, including teacher guides and videos, that integrate America's visual arts with history and literature. These materials are distributed to high school classrooms across the nation. This site provides information about these materials.

Notes:

_____

_____

_____

_____

National Endowment for the Arts

http://arts.endow.gov/

The National Endowment for the Arts is an independent agency of the Federal government charged with supporting the arts in America for all Americans.

Notes:

_____

_____

_____

_____

National Museum of American Art

http://www.nmaa.si.edu/

From the Smithsonian, the National Museum of American Art offers many online exhibition tours, including an impressive tour of the Ashcan artists and The White House Collection of American Crafts. Categories: Research Resources, Artworks, Education, Publications, and more

Notes:

_____

_____

_____

_____

The Refrigerator

http://www.seeusa.com/refrigerator.html

At this site kids can cast a vote for their favorite picture or submit their own artwork.

Notes:

_____

_____

_____

_____

Teacher's Guide for the Professional Cartoonist

http://www.cagle.com/teacher/

With helpful hints and lesson plans on how to use the Professional Cartoonists Index Web site **http://www.cagle.com/** in the classroom, this is a very interesting use of online information for the classroom.

Notes:

_____

_____

_____

_____

Web Museum

http://sunsite.unc.edu/wm/

A first stop for anyone looking for museum-quality art on the Web, this site features rotating exhibits from the likes of Cezanne, da Vinci, and David. The Famous Paintings section contains thousands of examples of the most well-known Western and Japanese art, from Gothic to Pop and everything in between. Categories: Many painters, Tour of Paris, Auditorium (Music)

Notes:

_____

_____

_____

_____

World Wide Art Resources

http://wwar.com/

At this one-stop resource for anyone interested in art resources on the Web, find over 3,000 categories, including an excellent list of online art museums and exhibitions.

Notes:

_____

_____

_____

_____

Classroom and Behavior Management

50 Tips on Classroom Management for ADD

http://www.chadd.org/50class.htm

This well-written and easy-to-read paper details strategies teachers can use to manage the classroom effectively for students with ADD.

Notes:

_____

_____

_____

_____

Behavior Home Page

http://www.state.ky.us/agencies/behave/homepage.html

From the Kentucky Department of Education, this site provides information on managing classroom behavior and tips and strategies for effective interventions.

Notes:

_____

_____

_____

_____

Behavior Management Frequently Asked Questions

http://www.bubbaonline.com

An easy-to-read question-and-answer type document discusses the pros and cons and the concerns and benefits of behavior management.

Notes:

_____

_____

_____

_____

Behavioral Research and Teaching

http://brt.uoregon.edu/

The Behavioral Research and Teaching working group combines applied behavior analysis with effective teaching practices to develop, study, and disseminate empirically-based educational programs for students who are at-risk in school and community. Categories: Behavior Disorders Program, Research Consultation and Teaching, Publications

Notes:

_____

_____

_____

_____

Classroom Discipline Techniques

http://users.aol.com/churchward/hls/techniques.html

Adapted from an article in Phi Delta Kappan, this page offers 11 strategies designed to promote effective interaction between students and teachers.

Notes:

_____

_____

_____

_____

Classroom Management (Teachers Helping Teachers)

http://www.pacificnet.net/~mandel/ClassroomManagement.html

The many suggestions from practicing teachers on different methods of classroom management and how to implement them are applicable to all grades.

Notes:

_____

_____

_____

_____

Classroom Management from Teachnet.com

http://www.teachnet.com/manage.html

A long article contains other articles and advice related to classroom management.

Notes:

_____

_____

_____

_____

Classroom Management of Attention Deficits

http://www.Webcom.com/rusleepy/articles/101tips.html

101 tips (102, actually) explain the techniques teachers can utilize when teaching students with attention deficit disorder.

Notes:

_____

_____

_____

_____

Classroom Management Special Education

http://www.pacificnet.net/~mandel/SpecialEducation.html

Many suggestions from practicing teachers (from the Teachers Helping Teachers site) detail different methods of classroom management and how to implement them (applicable to all grades).

Notes:

_____

_____

_____

_____

Honor Level System

http://members.aol.com/churchward/hls/index.html

This site presents The Honor Level System: Discipline by Design, a five-part series that details the benefits of the honor level system and how a teacher would implement it in the classroom; also included are the 11 techniques for better classroom discipline.

Notes:

_____

_____

_____

_____

Metamorphosis of Classroom Management

http://www.mcrel.org/products/noteworthy/franm.html

This article examines recent changes in the classroom management field and provides concrete examples of new approaches.

Notes:

_____

_____

_____

_____

Organization and Management of the Classroom

http://para.unl.edu/ServedDocuments/Organization/Intro.html

Part of a Web site for paraprofessionals, this is a chapter of an online book that covers classroom organization, rules and procedures, information on how to work with small groups, as well as lessons, activities, and even tests.

Notes:

_____

_____

_____

_____

Teacher's Encyclopedia of Behavior Management

http://www.state.ky.us/agencies/behave/encyndex.html

Two problem behaviors (aggression-verbal and/or physical and chaos/classroom out of control) and plans to intervene and correct the behaviors are addressed here by Dr. Randall Sprick.

Notes:

_____

_____

_____

_____

Teachers Helping Teachers—Classroom Management

http://www.pacificnet.net/~mandel/ClassroomManagement.html

Many tips and lesson plans are dedicated to classroom management from the Teachers Helping Teachers site. For Special Education tips, go here:
http://www.pacificnet.net/~mandel/SpecialEducation.html

Notes:

_____

_____

_____

_____

Using the Computer for Classroom Management
http://206.252.190.23/tips/manage.html

This site lists 10 ways that teachers can use the computer for classroom management issues and includes general methods and detailed information about their implementation.

Notes:

_____

_____

_____

_____

What Is Your Classroom Management Profile?
http://education.indiana.edu/cas/tt/v1i2/what.html

Take this very interesting online quiz that uses your responses to determine whether your style is authoritarian, authoritative, laissez-faire, or indifferent. Also, information is provided about each of the different styles.

Notes:

_____

_____

_____

_____

Diversity in the Classroom

African-American Mosaic

http://lcWeb.loc.gov/exhibits/african/intro.html

From the Library of Congress comes an online exhibition that explores the study of black history and culture. The information on colonization, abolition, migration, and the WPA includes ex-slave narratives.

Notes:

_____

_____

_____

_____

America's Life Histories—Manuscripts from the Federal Writer's Project

http://lcWeb2.loc.gov/ammem/wpaintro/wpahome.html

The Federal Writer's Project was a Depression-era government plan that put writers to work chronicling the history of the country in the words of those who lived it. This site contains thousands of interviews done for this project.

Notes:

_____

_____

_____

_____

Band-Aids and Blackboards

http://funrsc.fairfield.edu/~jfleitas/contents.html

This site is dedicated to sensitizing children to what it's like to grow up with a medical problem. Categories: Information for Kids, Teens, and Adults

Notes:

_____

_____

_____

_____

Clearinghouse for Multicultural/Bilingual Education

http://www.Weber.edu/MBE/htmls/mbe.html#main.index

The purpose of this Web site is to provide educators, pre-kindergarten to higher education, with commercial and non-commercial sources for multicultural and bilingual/ESL information, materials, and resources. Categories: Art, Books, Health, Institutions, Multimedia, Music, Periodicals, Professional Development, Resource Guides, Organizations, Teaching Aids

Notes:

_____

_____

_____

_____

Cradleboard Teaching Project

http://www.cradleboard.org/

Although parts of this site require a subscription and parts are hard to navigate, there remains enough information about the project for it to be worthwhile. It also includes an excellent list of Web resources.

Notes:

_____

_____

_____

_____

Encyclopedia of Women's History

http://www.teleport.com/~megaines/women.html

This interesting site showcases student work on famous (and not-so-famous) women. This site is a good showcase for what teachers can do with the Web, while it also offers information from and for students K–12. Submissions from students are accepted.

Notes:

_____

_____

_____

_____

Equity and Cultural Diversity

http://eric-Web.tc.columbia.edu/equity/

This good site features essays, digests, parent guides, and ERIC information alerts about equity and cultural diversity.

Notes:

_____

_____

_____

_____

_____

First Nations Histories

http://dickshovel.netgate.net/Compacts.html

This geographic overview of more than 40 Native American nations is very detailed, and though it lacks numerous graphics, this is an excellent resource.

Notes:

_____

_____

_____

_____

_____

Foreign Language Links

http://www.geocities.com/~lagringa

This huge site features categorized lists of links to many different foreign language pages on the Web, as well as international newspapers and magazines.

Notes:

_____

_____

_____

_____

Fourth World Documentation Project

http://www.halcyon.com/FWDP/fwdp.html

The goal of the Center for World Indigenous Studies is to present documents and resources related to the nations of the Fourth World. Categories: African Documents; European and Asian Documents; North, Central, and South American Documents; Treaties; United Nations Documents; and more

Notes:

_____

_____

_____

_____

Intercultural E-Mail Classroom Connections

http://www.stolaf.edu/network/iecc/

The IECC (Intercultural E-Mail Classroom Connections) mailing lists are provided by St. Olaf College as a free service to help teachers and classes link with partners in other countries and cultures for e-mail, classroom pen pals, and project exchanges.

Notes:

_____

_____

_____

_____

K–12 Electronic Guide for African Resources on the Internet

http://www.sas.upenn.edu/African_Studies/Home_Page/AFR_GIDE.html

The aim of this guide is to assist K–12 teachers, librarians, and students in locating online resources on Africa that can be used in the classroom for research and studies. This guide summarizes some relevant materials for K–12 uses available on the African Studies WWW. Categories: K–12 Information, Country-Specific Information, Multimedia, Environment

Notes:

_____

_____

_____

Martin Luther King, Jr.

http://www.seattletimes.com/mlk/index.html

From the *Seattle Times*, this in-depth look at the life and impact of Martin Luther King, Jr. is full of details and descriptions. Included are sound clips of the "I Have A Dream" and "Promised Land" speeches—a very good site.

Notes:

_____

_____

_____

_____

Multicultural Pavilion

http://curry.edschool.virginia.edu/go/multicultural/

This site strives to provide resources for educators to explore and discuss multicultural education and to facilitate opportunities for educators to work toward self-awareness and development. Categories: Resources for Teachers, Publications, Research and Inquiry, Discussion Board, and more

Notes:

_____

_____

_____

_____

National Association for Multicultural Education

http://www.inform.umd.edu/CampusInfo/Committees/Assoc/NAME/

The National Association for Multicultural Education (NAME) was founded in 1991 to bring together professionals from all academic disciplines and from diverse educational institutions, organizations, and occupations who had an interest in multicultural education.

Notes:

_____

_____

_____

_____

National Civil Rights Museum

http://www.mecca.org/~crights/

The National Civil Rights Museum presents a virtual tour of the civil rights movement in the 1960s. The site is nicely designed and informative, but other than the tour there isn't much content.

Notes:

_____

_____

_____

_____

Native American Schools, Student Groups, and Related Programs on the Internet

http://hanksville.phast.umass.edu/misc/NAschools.html

It contains links to just about everything you need to know about Native Americans as related to education. Categories: FAQ, Teachers' Resources, Native American K-12 Schools, Colleges, Native American Student Resources

Notes:

_____

_____

_____

_____

Slave Voices

http://odyssey.lib.duke.edu/slavery/

From the Special Collections Library of Duke University, the story of slavery is retold with the documents of the period. Bills of sale, newspaper advertisements, diaries, etc., are reproduced and interpreted—a very good site.

Notes:

_____

_____

_____

_____

Education, Laws, Regulations, and Standards

Americans with Disabilities Act

http://www.bubbaonline.com

You can find here the full text of the Americans with Disabilities Act.

Notes:

_____

_____

_____

_____

Developing Educational Standards

http://putwest.boces.org/Standards.html

This very extensive site catalogues nationwide educational standards, initiatives, and curriculum framework documents. Categories: Governments, organizations, periodicals, standards, and frameworks by subject area and states

Notes:

_____

_____

_____

_____

EdLaw

http://www.edlaw.net

Laws and other documents related to education are contained at this very extensive and well-maintained site. Note: The address of this site will be changing to www.edlaw.net. Categories: IDEA Regulations, Rehabilitation Act of 1973, Family Educational Rights and Privacy Act, Related Education Resources

Notes:

_____

_____

_____

_____

Goals 2000

http://www.ed.gov/pubs/goals/progrpt/index.html

The full Goals 2000 text, along with progress reports, clarifications, and addresses for contacts in every state can be found here. Categories: Grant Award Information, Reform efforts, Conditions for Learning, Misconceptions, State Contacts

Notes:

_____

_____

_____

_____

Internet Law Library

http://law.house.gov/

A free service of the U.S. House of Representatives, this site features an exhaustive list of federal and state laws, available in full. It even includes the constitutions and laws of other nations and hundreds of treaties and other international laws.

Notes:

_____

_____

_____

_____

_____

Model Content Standards for Curriculum—Mathematics

http://cdp.mde.state.mi.us/MCF/ContentStandards/mathematics/default.html

The state's Math Curriculum Standards are at this site.

Notes:

_____

_____

_____

_____

_____

Model Content Standards for Curriculum—Science

http://cdp.mde.state.mi.us/MCF/ContentStandards/science/default.html

The state's Science Curriculum Standards are given here.

Notes:

_____

_____

_____

_____

_____

_____

Model Content Standards for Curriculum—Social Studies

http://cdp.mde.state.mi.us/MCF/ContentStandards/socialstudies/default.html

Find the state's Social Studies Curriculum Standards here.

Notes:

_____

_____

_____

_____

_____

_____

National Science Education Standards

http://www.nap.edu/readingroom/books/nses/

Find the standards providing specific guidelines on content, teaching, professional development, and assessment of science education programs and systems.

Notes:

_____

_____

_____

_____

National Standards for Art Education

gopher://gopher.ed.gov/11/publications/full_text/arts

Available online and as a downloadable Zip file, the NSAE was developed by the Consortium of National Arts Education Associations and titled "What Every Young American Should Know and Be Able to Do in the Arts."

Notes:

_____

_____

_____

_____

National Standards for Physical Education

http://www.aahperd.org/naspe/stdspe.html

Listed is the full text of the National Standards for Physical Education, including samples for grades four and eight.

Notes:

_____

_____

_____

_____

_____

National Standards for School Health Education

http://www.ericsp.org/news2.html

Developed by the Joint Committee for National School Health Education Standards (1995), this page is the full text of the standards.

Notes:

_____

_____

_____

_____

_____

National Standards for United States History

http://www.sscnet.ucla.edu/nchs/

At this site are the complete national standards for U.S. History for grades K–4 and 5–12 and the national standards for world history.

Notes:

_____

_____

_____

_____

_____

Regulations Implementing IDEA
(34 C.F.R. Part 300)

http://www.edlaw.net/public/iep_cont.htm

Full text of the Individuals with Disabilities Education Act includes a hyperlinked outline that lets you jump within sections.

Notes:

_____

_____

_____

_____

_____

Standards for Foreign Language Learning

http://www.educ.iastate.edu/currinst/nflrc/stds.pub.html#stan

This site provides the full text of the Standards for Foreign Language Learning and also includes a guide for aligning curriculum with the standards.

Notes:

_____

_____

_____

_____

_____

Unites States Code

http://www.law.cornell.edu/uscode/

Within a searchable digital file of the complete U.S. laws from Cornell University is the section on Education which is informative without being overwhelming. This is a well-designed and comprehensive site.

Notes:

_____

_____

_____

_____

_____

Environment

American Farmland Trust

http://www.farmland.org/

This organization dedicated to preserving America's farmland provides good information on the effects of urban sprawl. Categories: Tools, Policy, News, Publications, and Merchandise

Notes:

_____

_____

_____

_____

EE-Link Environmental Education on the Internet

http://www.nceet.snre.umich.edu/index.html

A project of the National Consortium for Environmental Education and Training, this site contains many classroom resources, including online lessons, a great image gallery, and references to other environmental information.

Notes:

_____

_____

_____

_____

Environmental News Network

http://www.enn.com/

Environmental News Network produces high quality, moderated content (stories, radio broadcasts, etc.) related to environmental and science topics. One of the best environmental sites.

Notes:

_____

_____

_____

_____

Greenpeace

http://www.greenpeace.org/index.shtml

Greenpeace, the major player in environmental activism, has compiled a resource-rich site full of late-breaking news, in-depth stories, press releases, and an excellent multimedia archive of pictures, movies, and sounds.

Notes:

_____

_____

_____

_____

National Wildlife Federation

http://www.nwf.org/

This very deep site offers mounds of information on almost every imaginable environmental topic. Resources for teachers include lesson plans and information about environmental workshops. Categories: Issues, Environmental Education, Magazines and Publications, Collaborative Conservatism, and Just for Kids

Notes:

_____

_____

_____

_____

U.S. Environmental Protection Agency

http://www.epa.gov

A very extensive site, it contains almost any bit of information you want on the government's efforts to protect the environment. For teachers there are curriculum guides, and for students there are fact sheets on various environmental issues.

Notes:

_____

_____

_____

_____

U.S. Global Change Data

http://www.gcdis.usgcrp.gov/

A collection of distributed information systems operated by government agencies involved in global change research, GCDIS provides global change data to scientists and researchers, policy makers, educators, industry, and the public at large.

Notes:

_____

_____

_____

_____

_____

_____

_____

_____

_____

_____

_____

_____

_____

_____

_____

_____

Funding Sources

Alfred P. Sloan Foundation

http://www.sloan.org/

A very well-known source of grant and other funding opportunities, the Sloan Foundation awarded over $35 million in 1996 alone. Their five primary interests are 1. Science and Technology, 2. Standard of Living and Economic Performance, 3. Education and Careers in Science and Technology, 4. Selected National Issues, and 5. Civic Projects. This site contains all the information needed to apply for a grant.

Notes:

_____

_____

_____

Carnegie Corporation

http://www.carnegie.org/

Although the Carnegie Corporation does not usually give grants to individuals (there are some exceptions), they do make many grants to academic institutions and other professional organizations. This site lists all you need to know to apply. Categories: Information, Restrictions and Proposals, Recent Grants, Corporation News

Notes:

_____

_____

_____

Electronic Learning

http://place.scholastic.com/el/grants/gropen.htm

From *Electronic Learning* magazine, an updated list of open grant opportunities related to technology in the classroom provides a description of the grant and contact information. Also included is other grant-related information.

Notes:

_____

_____

_____

_____

FEDIX

http://Web.fie.com/htdoc/fed/all/any/any/menu/any/index.htm

FEDIX is a free one-stop information retrieval service of federal opportunities for the education and research communities. You can register to receive free e-mail notifications of upcoming opportunities here:

http://nscp.fie.com/wincgi/fed/all/any/any/foa/any/keywords.exe/Menu

Notes:

_____

_____

_____

_____

Fulbright Grants

http://www.cies.org/

The U.S. Congress created the Fulbright Program in 1946, immediately after World War II, to foster mutual understanding among nations through educational and cultural exchanges. This site from the Council for International Exchange of Scholars gives information on the program, how to obtain an application, and an overview of the selection process. Categories: General Information, Grant Opportunities, Participants, Application Request

Notes:

_____

_____

_____

_____

Grantmaker Information

http://fdncenter.org/grantmaker/contents. html

Provided here are pointers to many other grant resources on the Web as well as guides and brochures on producing effective grant proposals—another very useful site. Categories: Links, Informational Materials

Notes:

_____

_____

_____

Grants and (Other) People's Money

http://quest.arc.nasa.gov/top/grants.html

Focusing on science, math, engineering, and educational technology, this excellent resource for grant seekers was produced as part of NASA's K–12 Internet Initiative. Categories: Grant News, Organizations Offering Grants, Links

Notes:

_____

_____

_____

_____

Grants Net—Department of Health and Human Services

http://www.os.dhhs.gov/progorg/grantsnet/index.html

Grants Net is a tool for finding and exchanging information about HHS and selected other federal grant programs. It is part of the much-publicized national movement toward providing government resources to the general public in a more accessible and meaningful manner. Categories: How to Find Grant Information, Search for Funding, Links, Administering Grants

Notes:

_____

_____

_____

_____

GrantsWeb

http://Web.fie.com/cws/sra/resource.htm

A huge site provides lots of information on grants and other funding opportunities from government and private organizations. Categories: Government Resources, Policy Information and Circulars, General Resources, Private Funding Resources, Links

Notes:

_____

_____

_____

_____

IRIS Funding Opportunities

http://carousel.lis.uiuc.edu/~iris/search.html

In this searchable database of over 7,000 grants, you can search by keyword, deadline date, or sponsor name. It is updated daily by the sponsors.

Notes:

_____

_____

_____

_____

National Science Foundation Grant Opportunities

http://www.nsf.gov/home/grants.htm

This section of the NSF's site is devoted to grant opportunities and provides a searchable database of grant opportunities and information on how to apply. Categories: Funding Opportunities, Proposal Preparation, Award Administration, Award Data, Contracts

Notes:

_____

_____

_____

_____

Research Sponsors

http://www.cs.virginia.edu/research/sponsors. html

From the University of Virginia comes a very extensive list of government, public, and private organizations where funding can be obtained for educational projects. Categories: Government Agencies, Foundations and Associations, Links

Notes:

_____

_____

_____

_____

Resource Guide to Federal Funding For Technology in Education

http://www.ed.gov/Technology/tec-guid.html

An excellent guide to grant opportunities related to technology within the federal government, this site includes descriptions of grants, contact numbers, and much more.

Notes:

_____

_____

_____

_____

_____

Resources for Grant Writers on the Internet

http://chroma.med.miami.edu/research/UMich_Resources_for_Grant.html

A plain but very useful site, it details online resources for grant writers.

Notes:

_____

_____

_____

_____

_____

Tips for Writing Grant Proposals

http://www.ascd.org/services/grantinfo/tips.html

Provided by The Association for Supervision and Curriculum Development are a few tips to follow when developing proposals.

Notes:

_____

_____

_____

_____

_____

U.S. Department of Education Grants and Contracts Information

http://gcs.ed.gov/

Featured are constantly updated information about grants available from the U.S. Department of Education, grant requirements, and application procedures.

Notes:

_____

_____

_____

_____

_____

What Should I Know About ED Grants?

http://www.ed.gov/pubs/KnowAbtGrants/

Presented in an easy-to-understand Q & A format, this site from the U.S. Department of Education is an online paper that explains the grant process within the D.O.E.

Notes:

_____

_____

_____

_____

_____

Who's Who in Federal Grant Management

http://www.hhs.gov/progorg/grantsnet/whoswho.html

This directory of key contacts in federal grant management includes names, phone numbers, and e-mail addresses.

Notes:

_____

_____

_____

_____

_____

General Educational Aids

Apple Education Worldwide

http://www.apple.com/education/

Apple's education Web site features tons of useful information for students, teachers, and parents. It is a little heavy on the Apple propaganda, but still a good site.

Notes:

_____

_____

_____

_____

Busy Teacher's K-12 Website

http://www.ceismc.gatech.edu/BusyT/

This is a very big information site. Hundreds of links in a very well-organized format point you to sites ranging from archaeology to social studies. Categories: Archaeology, Art, Astronomy, Biology, Chemistry, Ecology, Elementary School, English, Geology, History, Math, Paleontology, Physics, Recess, Reference, Science, Social Studies, Technology

Notes:

_____

_____

_____

_____

Carrie's Sites for Educators

http://www.mtjeff.com/~bodenst/page5.html

This a page of links for educators is divided by academic discipline, not annotated but still useful and growing all the time. Categories: Search Engines, General Education, Counseling and Guidance, Humanities, Social Studies, Science, Math, Internet

Notes:

_____

_____

_____

_____

The Chalkboard

http://thechalkboard.com/

At this site find information on education programs, grants, scholarships, services, and curriculum. You can search by subject, grade level, and geographic area.

Notes:

_____

_____

_____

_____

Collaborative Learning

http://www.moostuff.force9.co.uk/

Find information about collaborative learning, including how to set up small groups, research on the subject, and related links.

Notes:

_____

_____

_____

_____

_____

Daily Report Cards

http://commons.utopia.usweb.com/mailings/reportcard/index.html

---

A summary of news in K–12 education, this site recently cut back to thrice weekly and comes out of the National Education Goals Panel.

Notes:

_____

_____

_____

_____

_____

Education Free Forum

http://www.edforum.com/

Offering daily news for administrators, teachers, parents, and students, this site also contains archived issues, teaching and lesson tips, and free offers (catalogs, software, etc.).

Notes:

_____

_____

_____

_____

_____

Games Kids Play

http://www.corpcomm.net/~gnieboer/gamehome.htm

Here are hundreds of ideas to fill that half hour of physical education. Also included are game descriptions, rules, and objectives.

Notes:

_____

_____

_____

_____

_____

Home School Resource Center

http://www.rsts.net/home/home.html

Featuring a huge list of related links, The Home School Resource Center is a good first stop if you're looking for information on home schooling. Categories: Links, Curriculum, E-Pals, Legal, Socialization

Notes:

_____

_____

_____

_____

Intercultural E-Mail Classroom Connections

http://www.stolaf.edu/network/iecc/

The IECC (Intercultural E-Mail Classroom Connections) mailing lists are provided by St. Olaf College as a free service to help teachers and classes link with partners in other countries and cultures for e-mail classroom pen-pal and project exchanges.

Notes:

_____

_____

_____

_____

International WWW Schools Registry

http://Web66.coled.umn.edu/schools.html

This site attempts to keep an updated list of all the schools in the world that have a home page on the Web. These are very interesting sites, and it's just fun for kids or anyone else to visit these classrooms and see how they're studying geography in Portugal or computers in Senegal.

Notes:

_____

_____

_____

_____

KidsConnect

http://www.ala.org/ICONN/AskKC.html

This site allows children to ask for information on any topic and receive an e-mailed response within 48 hours. Great for reports, science projects, and any fact-finding mission.

Notes:

_____

_____

_____

_____

New Teacher Page

http://www.geocities.com/Athens/Delphi/7862/

The New Teacher Page is a resource site for education students, student teachers, first-year teachers, teacher certification candidates, and those who think maybe, just maybe, they'd like to be educators someday. Categories: All About Teaching, Becoming a Teacher, Finding a Job, First Year Resources, Substitute Teaching, and Your Classroom

Notes:

_____

_____

_____

PBS Learn With PBS

http://www.pbs.org/learn/

This site serves as a front-line resource for PBS member stations, supplying information and support services for the effective use of K–12 educational television and related technology. Provides information about instructional television. Categories: Electronic Field Trips, Teacher Connect, Mathline, Scienceline, Ready to Learn

Notes:

_____

_____

_____

PBS Online

http://www.pbs.org/

The home page for PBS offers many educational resources, as well as information about PBS programs.

Notes:

_____

_____

_____

_____

_____

Pedago Net

http://www.pedagonet.com/

This is an online "classifieds" section that lets teachers buy and sell learning resources. Four-day postings are free.

Notes:

_____

_____

_____

_____

Teacher Exchange Register

http://www.ats.com.au/~hoddo/

The Teacher Exchange Register aims to allow teachers throughout the world to establish contact with each other in order to find suitable matches for a possible teaching exchange.

Notes:

_____

_____

_____

_____

Teacher Magazine

http://www.edweek.org/tm/tm.htm

Part of the Education Week on the Web site, *Teacher Magazine* is a slick, very informative online magazine. Changes are made weekly. Categories: Current Events, Research (Policy and Findings), Editorials, Features (full text)

Notes:

_____

_____

_____

_____

Teacher Talk

http://education.indiana.edu/cas/tt/tthmpg.html

Teacher Talk is published by the Center for Adolescent Studies at the School of Education, Indiana University, Bloomington, IN. It is a publication for preservice secondary education teachers.

Notes:

_____

_____

_____

_____

Teacher Tips

http://www.epix.net/~cyndilou/tips.htm

This site offers ideas about classroom management, positive reinforcement, jobs for students in your classroom, writing starters, words of wisdom, lesson plans, assessment ideas, a story map to assist your students, and much more.

Notes:

_____

_____

_____

_____

Teacher's Center

http://www.eduplace.com/teacher/index.html

From Houghton Mifflin, this site offers collaborative project ideas, discussion forums, and information on math, language arts, and social studies.

Notes:

_____

_____

_____

_____

_____

Teacher's Edition Online (Teachnet.com)

http://www.teachnet.com/

A very good place for teachers to search for instruction ideas, the site also includes lesson plans, information on classroom management, humorous articles and anecdotes, and a lot more—a very extensive site. Categories: Teacher-2-Teacher, Lesson Ideas Resources & Links, How To, EdNews from the Web

Notes:

_____

_____

_____

_____

Teachers Helping Teachers

http://www.pacificnet.net/~mandel/

A private site, this one offers teachers the opportunity to exchange tips about instruction, classroom management, and anything else that goes on in the classroom.

Notes:

_____

_____

_____

_____

_____

_____

_____

_____

_____

_____

_____

_____

_____

_____

_____

_____

_____

_____

_____

Geography

Atlapedia Online

http://www.atlapedia.com/index.html

Atlapedia Online contains key information on every country of the world. Each country profile provides facts and data on geography, climate, people, religion, language, history, and economy, making it ideal for personal or family education and students of all ages.

Notes:

_____

_____

_____

_____

CIA World Fact Book

http://www.odci.gov/cia/publications/nsolo/wfb-all.htm

Proving that the Cold War is really over, the CIA has put online an incredible resource for students and teachers (and anyone interested in other countries). From Afghanistan to Zimbabwe, and all countries in between, a wealth of facts is at your fingertips.

Notes:

_____

_____

_____

_____

Country Studies from the Library of Congress

http://lcWeb2.loc.gov/frd/cs/cshome.html

Part of the Library of Congress Web site, 71 different country studies are provided with more being added all the time. These are very, very extensive studies with much more than you'll probably need to know, but they are well-designed and easy to navigate.

Notes:

_____

_____

_____

_____

50 States and Capitals

http://www.scvol.com/States/main.htm

An excellent resource if you need to plan a lesson on Michigan or any of the other 49 states, it contains interesting and sometimes humorous information about all the states.

Notes:

_____

_____

_____

_____

Geography Education from National Geographic

http://www.nationalgeographic.com/resources/ngo/education/

Many lesson plans and classroom ideas are included, and also featured are a
geography discussion forum, many maps, and information on the geography bee.

Notes:

_____

_____

_____

_____

_____

Map Machine (National Geographic)

http://www.nationalgeographic.com/resources/ngo/maps/

With excellent maps of the world and of individual countries, this site also offers
flags, facts, and profiles of the countries of the world and each U.S. state.

Notes:

_____

_____

_____

_____

_____

Mapquest

http://www.mapquest.com/

At this site are street maps from all over the world and an interactive trip atlas. Tell it where you are starting from and where you want to go, and it will tell you how to get there. The Tripquest section is especially useful.

Notes:

_____

_____

_____

_____

_____

National Geographic Magazine

http://www.nationalgeographic.com/main.html

The online home of *National Geographic* requires free registration and offers a lot, including places for kids, full-length articles, and pictures galore.

Notes:

_____

_____

_____

_____

Government

Federal Offices Department of Defense

http://www.odedodea.edu/

Find at the home page for the Department of Defense Education Activity schools and programs, personnel and management services, current events, and pages by students, teachers, and alumni. You can also visit some DoDEA districts.

Notes:

_____

_____

_____

_____

Department of Education

http://www.ed.gov

The home page for the Department of Education includes information on the Secretary's Initiatives. The site is updated regularly with the latest education news, both good and bad, and all the federal school information you could ask for. Categories: Secretary's Initiatives, Programs & Services, Publications & Products, People & Offices, News, FAQs, Money Matters, Links

Notes:

_____

_____

_____

_____

Department of Education Grants and Contracts Information

http://gcs.ed.gov/

This site provides constantly updated information about grants available from the U.S Department of Education, grant requirements, and application procedures.

Notes:

_____

_____

_____

_____

Department of Health and Human Services

http://www.hhs.gov/

The Department of Health and Human Services is the United States government's principal agency for protecting the health of all Americans and providing essential human services, especially for those who are least able to help themselves.

Notes:

_____

_____

_____

_____

Environmental Protection Agency

http://www.epa.gov

A very extensive site, it contains almost any bit of information you want on the government's efforts to protect the environment. For teachers, there are curriculum guides, and for students there are fact sheets on various environmental aspects.

Notes:

_____

_____

_____

_____

House of Representatives

http://www.house.gov/

This very good educational resources section provides up-to-the-minute news on House happenings, committee schedules, and links to all of the representatives.

Notes:

_____

_____

_____

_____

Library of Congress

http://marvel.loc.gov/

From the biggest library in the world comes perhaps one of the best Web sites ever. Search for legislative information, browse exhibits, or use their research search tool to search other Internet sites. Categories: Search Engines, Special Exhibits, News and Events, National Library Service for the Blind and Physically Handicapped

Notes:

_____

_____

_____

_____

National Archives and Records Administration

http://www.nara.gov/

An excellent government site features educational resources in the digital classroom. Teachers can use archived records for classroom exercises and can take advantage of online lesson plans.

Notes:

_____

_____

_____

_____

National Center for Education Statistics
http://NCES.ed.gov/

The National Center for Education Statistics fulfills a Congressional mandate to collect, collate, analyze, and report complete statistics on the condition of American education; conduct and publish reports; and review and report on education activities internationally. Categories: Education at a Glance, FAQ, NCES Publications, Links

Notes:

_____

_____

_____

_____

National Science Foundation
http://www.nsf.gov/

Including everything you need to know about the NSF, this site is devoted to fostering science and engineering research and education. Categories: Biology, Geosciences, Math, Physical Sciences, Education, Engineering, Polar Research, Links

Notes:

_____

_____

_____

_____

Office of Elementary and Secondary Education Programs

http://www.ed.gov/pubs/TeachersGuide/oese.html

Part of the Teacher's Guide to the U.S. Department of Education, this section covers the Office of Elementary and Secondary Education Programs.

Notes:

_____

_____

_____

_____

_____

Office of Postsecondary Education Programs

http://www.ed.gov/pubs/TeachersGuide/opep.html

Part of the Teacher's Guide to the U.S. Department of Education, this section covers the Office of Postsecondary Education Programs.

Notes:

_____

_____

_____

_____

_____

Office of Special Education and Rehabilitative Services Programs Teacher's Guide

http://www.ed.gov/pubs/TeachersGuide/osers.html

Part of the Teacher's Guide to the U.S. Department of Education, this section covers the Office of Special Education and Rehabilitative Services Program.

Notes:

_____

_____

_____

_____

Office of Special Education Programs

http://www.ed.gov/offices/OSERS/OSEP/index.html

OSEP's mission and organization focus on the free appropriate public education of children and youth with disabilities from birth through age 21 and features funding information, reports, and links.

Notes:

_____

_____

_____

_____

Senate

http://www.senate.gov

Take a virtual tour of the Senate, learn about its history, or read the recent legislation under consideration.

Notes:

_____

_____

_____

_____

_____

White House

http://www.whitehouse.gov/WH/Welcome.html

This very heavily visited site has information on the current and past occupants, news releases, and an excellent virtual library.

Notes:

_____

_____

_____

_____

_____

State Departments of Education

Alabama
http://www.alsde.edu/

Alaska
http://www.educ.state.ak.us/

Arizona
http://www.acpe.asu.edu/

Arkansas
http://arkedu.k12.ar.us/

California
http://goldmine.cde.ca.gov/

Colorado
http://www.cde.state.co.us/

Connecticut
http://www.aces.k12.ct.us/

Delaware
http://www.dpi.state.de.us/

District of Columbia
http://www.k12.dc.us/

Florida
http://www.firn.edu/doe/

Georgia
http://www.doe.k12.ga.us

Hawaii
http://www.k12.hi.us/

Idaho
http://www2.state.id.us/

Illinois
http://www.isbe.state.il.us

Indiana
http://www.doe.state.in.us/

Iowa
http://www.state.ia.us/educate/depteduc/index.html

Kansas
http://www.ksbe.state.ks.us/

Kentucky
http://www.kde.state.ky.us/

Louisiana
http://www.doe.state.la.us/

Maine
http://www.state.me.us/education/homepage.htm

Maryland
http://www.mec.state.md.us/meceduc.html

Massachusetts
http://info.doe.mass.edu/

Michigan
http://www.mde.state.mi.us/

Minnesota
http://www.educ.state.mn.us/

Mississippi
http://mdek12.state.ms.us/

State Departments of Education *(cont.)*

Missouri
http://services.dese.state.mo.us/

Montana
http://161.7.114.15/OPI/Main.html

Nebraska
http://www.nde.state.ne.us/

Nevada
http://www.nsn.k12.nv.us/nvdoe/

New Hampshire
http://www.state.nh.us/doe/education.html

New Jersey
http://www.state.nj.us/education/

New Mexico
http://sde.state.nm.us/

New York
http://www.nysed.gov/

North Carolina
http://www.dpi.state.nc.us/

North Dakota
http://www.dpi.state.nd.us

Ohio
http://www.ode.ohio.gov/

Oklahoma
http://sde.state.ok.us/

Oregon
http://www.ode.state.or.us//

Pennsylvania
http://www.cas.psu.edu/pde.html

Rhode Island
http://instruct.ride.ri.net/ride_home_page.html

South Carolina
http://www.state.sc.us/sde

South Dakota
http://www.state.sd.us/state/executive/deca/

Tennessee
http://www.state.tn.us/education/

Texas
http://www.tea.state.tx.us/

Utah
http://www.usoe.k12.ut.us/

Vermont
http://www.state.vt.us/educ/

Virginia
http://pen.k12.va.us/Anthology/VDOE/

Washington
http://www.ospi.wednet.edu/

West Virginia
http://wvde.state.wv.us/

Wisconsin
http://www.dpi.state.wi.us/

Wyoming
http://www.k12.wy.us/

Language Arts

Alphabet Superhighway

http://www.ash.udel.edu/ash/

The Alphabet Superhighway, under sponsorship of the U.S. Department of Education's READ*WRITE*NOW! Initiative, assists secondary and upper elementary students to create, locate, and communicate information through active learning, guided discovery, mentoring, competitions, and other online activities. Categories: Exhibit Hall, Cyberzine, Library, Challenge Chaser, Teachers' Lounge, Parents' Place

Notes:

American Literacy Classics-A Chapter A Day

http://www.americanliterature.com

This site features online books such as *The Wizard of Oz, Moby Dick,* and *The Red Badge of Courage* set up so that you can read a chapter a day. (Be warned, though, *Moby Dick* is 135 chapters long!). You can go to the site above for the current book or check out the archives section at:
http://www.americanliterature.com/ARCHIVES/ARCHIVES.HTML

Notes:

Banned Books

http://www.ala.org/bbooks/index.html

Part of the American Library Association's site, this page includes information about how books are banned, the most challenged and banned books, and the most challenged and banned authors in the U.S. for the last year.

Notes:

_____

_____

_____

_____

_____

Book Club

http://www.smplanet.com/bookclub/bookclub.html

Containing everything you need to know about starting a book club, this is a project done, in part, by MSU Teacher Education professor Taffy Raphael. Categories: Methodology, Materials, Forum, Author Information

Notes:

_____

_____

_____

_____

Book Nook

http://i-site.on.ca/booknook.html

I can't say enough about this one. Kids read books, then post their book reports here. This site is for any teacher who has ever had a student who asked, "Why do I have to write a book report?" The reports serve as a repository of information that kids can access to discover interesting books to read themselves. It is divided by grade level and searchable.

Notes:

_____

_____

_____

_____

Caldecott Medal Winners

http://www.bubbaonline.com/literacy.htm

Looking for a great book to read? You can't go wrong with any one of these. Since 1938, the American Library Association has awarded the Caldecott Medal to the most distinguished American picture book. Here's the complete list of winners.

Notes:

_____

_____

_____

_____

Children's Literature Web Guide

http://www.acs.ucalgary.ca/~dkbrown/index.html

This is one of the best education sites there is. There are more resources to literacy and children's reading than just about anywhere else. This has to be Canada's best educational site.

Notes:

_____

_____

_____

_____

Newbery Award Winners

http://www.bubbaonline.com/literacy.htm

This is a medal presented annually to the author of the most distinguished contribution to American literature for children published in the United States in the preceding year. The recipient must be a citizen or resident of the United States.

Notes:

_____

_____

_____

_____

Carol Hurst's Children's Literature Site

http://www.carolhurst.com

This site, sponsored in part by Teaching K–8 magazine, offers many resources about children's literature, not the least of these being lesson plans in U.S. history, geography, reading, writing, and science. Categories: Children's Books, Subjects in Children's Books, Professional Resources, Free Newsletter

Notes:

_____

_____

_____

_____

Bulwer-Lytton Fiction Contest

http://www.bulwer-lytton.com/

The site where WWW means Wretched Writers Welcome. Sponsored by the English Department at San Jose State University, the trick is to compose the opening sentence to the worst of all possible novels. Read the past winners' entries to see what never to do.

Notes:

_____

_____

_____

_____

Cool Word of the Day

http://130.63.218.180/~wotd/

Nobody said literacy couldn't be attained one word at a time. This site has, as the title says, a "cool" featured word of the day and also accepts submissions.

Notes:

Create Your Own Newspaper

http://crayon.net/

A free site, CRAYON lets kids (and adults) create their very own newspaper. With downloadable links to real newspaper and broadcast stories and graphics, this is a great place to experiment and learn the ins and outs of journalism.

Notes:

CyberSeuss

http://www.afn.org/~afn15301/drseuss.html

The home page of Dr. Seuss discusses everything about his life and work. As far as I can tell, none of the books are online (at least, none are authorized to be online). Still, there are some useful things here, and it's just interesting to read about the man who created the Lorax, Horton, and the Cat in the Hat.

Notes:

_____

_____

_____

_____

Disney's Storybooks

http://www.disney.com/DisneyBooks/new/StoryBook/StoryBook.html

Read Disney's "improved" serialized storybooks online, now featuring *The Hunchback of Notre Dame* and *Aladdin*. Each story includes big pictures and easy-to-read text.

Notes:

_____

_____

_____

_____

ESL Café Quote Page

http://www.pacificnet.net/~sperling/cookie.pl.cgi?

In this collection of quotes from around the world, a suggested activity is for students to find a quote they like and then write a short story about the moral or lesson to which the quote pertains. It is part of a larger site called Dave ESL Café: **http://www.pacificnet.net/~sperling/**. Categories: Bookstore, Graffiti Wall, Help Center, Job Center, Links for Teachers and Students, Quiz Center

Notes:

_____

_____

_____

Folk and Fairy Tales from Around the World

http://darsie.ucdavis.edu/tales/

A collection of folk fairy tales from many countries, this is an excellent site for students to explore to gain an understanding of the importance of folklore. "The stories in this collection represent a small sampling of the rich storytelling art that is the common heritage of humanity." Tales: Africa, Central Asia, Central Europe, China, England, India, Ireland, Japan, Middle East, Native America, Russia, Scandinavia, Scotland, Siberia

Notes:

_____

_____

_____

Foreign Language Links

http://www.geocities.com/~lagringa/

This huge site features categorized lists of links to many different foreign language pages on the Web, as well as international newspapers and magazines.

Notes:

_____

_____

_____

_____

_____

Grammar Lady

http://www.grammarlady.com/

The Grammar Lady answers grammar questions and posts online articles about grammar use (and misuse).

Notes:

_____

_____

_____

_____

_____

Grimm's Fairy Tales

gopher://ftp.std.com/11/obi/book/Fairy.Tales/Grimm

Although it is a very bare-bones site with no pictures, there are over 40 fairy tales that deserve rereading every so often. Complete text is available.

Notes:

_____

_____

_____

_____

International Reading Association

http://www.ira.org

The International Reading Association seeks to promote high levels of literacy for all by improving the quality of reading instruction through studying the reading process and teaching techniques; serving as a clearinghouse for the dissemination of reading research through conferences, journals, and other publications; and actively encouraging the lifetime reading habit. Categories: Conferences & Conventions, Councils & Affiliates, Publications, International Projects, Research, Advocacy

Notes:

_____

_____

_____

_____

Internet Wiretap

http://wiretap.area.com/

With many online books from Mark Twain to Jane Austen, the site also contains numerous government documents like international treaties and covenants, various constitutions, and U.S. government reports. Categories: Electronic Books, Government Documents, Online Library

Notes:

_____

_____

_____

ISN KidNews

http://www.vsa.cape.com/~powens/Kidnews3.html

This site is full of submissions from students and is an excellent place to publish your students' work and get ideas for new literacy projects. *KidNews* is a free news and writing service for students and teachers around the world. Anyone may use stories from the service for educational purposes, and anyone may submit stories. They also offer pen-pal services (parental permission required). Categories: News, Creative, Sports, Adults Talk, Kids Talk, Reviews, Links

Notes:

_____

_____

_____

Jesse's Word of the Day

http://www.randomhouse.com/jesse/

For literacy one word at a time, Jesse each day takes on the etymological derivations of English words and phrases.

Notes:

_____

_____

_____

_____

_____

Links to Electronic Book and Text Sites

http://www.awa.com/library/omnimedia/links.html

Just a simple page, it offers an up-to-date list of sites on the Web that offer electronic books and texts.

Notes:

_____

_____

_____

_____

_____

Literacy Resources on the Net

http://www.english.upenn.edu/~jlynch/Lit/

Almost anything you want to find about literacy is categorized (e.g., Renaissance, American, Theatre and Drama, Women's Literature, etc.)—a good place to start your research.

Notes:

_____

_____

_____

_____

National Center for the Study of Writing and Literacy

http://www-gse.berkeley.edu/research/NCSWL/csw.homepage.html

The mission of the Center is to improve understanding of how writing is best learned and taught from the early years through adulthood. The mission has been completed, but you can still read the research results here.

Notes:

_____

_____

_____

_____

National Council of Teachers of English

http://www.ncte.org/

Lots of resources for teachers include lesson plans and ideas on how to integrate language arts into other curriculum areas, and also featured is a discussion forum. Categories: Teaching Ideas, Professional Development, Publications, Positions, Grants, Conversations

Notes:

_____

_____

_____

_____

_____

The Online Books Page

http://www.cs.cmu.edu/bookauthors.html

A large, searchable list of online books can be found at this site.

Notes:

_____

_____

_____

_____

_____

Online English Grammar

http://www.Cue.uga.edu/Idcenter/

A great online grammar book, it is searchable alphabetically or by topic. Also featured are sound files for pronunciation rules.

Notes:

_____

_____

_____

_____

Project Gutenberg

http://promo.net/pg/index.html

Full of online books, short stories, government documents, etc., Project Gutenberg was originally conceived as a computer repository of printed material, and their database keeps growing and growing. This site is one of the reasons the Internet thrives. Categories: News, Links, Newsletters, Articles, E-text Listings

Notes:

_____

_____

_____

_____

Schoolhouse Rock

http://www.apocalypse.org/pub/u/gilly/Schoolhouse_Rock/HTML/schoolhouse.html

Ah, the 70s rear their collective head once again. Schoolhouse Rock, with its songs that are burned into the brain of everyone who grew up with Saturday morning cartoons in the 1970s, has a new Web site. Read (and listen to) all the Schoolhouse Rock songs, including grammar rock. Don't miss "Conjunction Junction." (It's got a nice beat, but you can't dance to it; I'd give it a 75, Mr. Clark.)

Notes:

_____

_____

_____

_____

Strunk's Elements of Style

http://www.columbia.edu/acis/bartleby/strunk/

The complete version of *Elements of Style*, the handbook of writers for decades, is presented in an easily "clickable" format.

Notes:

_____

_____

_____

_____

Lesson Plans

Educast

http://www.educast.com

This free service offers cross-curricular lesson plans, education news, and professional development information. You can specify your particular area of interest and have information sent directly to your computer.

Notes:

_____

_____

_____

_____

Houghton Mifflin Activity Search

http://www.eduplace.com/search/activity.html

Search by grade level and activity: Language Arts, Math, Social Studies, Science, and Art. You can also browse by theme.

Notes:

_____

_____

_____

_____

Learn2.com

http://www.learn2.com/browse/hear.html

A highly regarded site, it features online lessons in hundreds of topics from cleaning a stereo to learning French and Spanish. Categories: Food and Drink, Healthier Living, Hobbies, Communication, Finance, Childcare, Cleaning, Computers, Automotive, and more

Notes:

_____

_____

_____

_____

Lesson Plans by Content Area

http://www.iglou.com/wcet/edtech/currlink/lesson.htm

This site provides a categorized list of links to lesson plan resources on the Internet. Categories: English and Writing, General, History, Math, Physical Education & Health, Science, and Special Needs

Notes:

_____

_____

_____

_____

Teachnet.com

http://www.teachnet.com/

Many lesson plans are provided by teachers in a variety of categories: art, health/physical education, Internet, music, language, math, science, social studies, and miscellaneous.

Notes:

_____

_____

_____

_____

_____

_____

_____

_____

_____

_____

_____

_____

_____

_____

_____

_____

_____

_____

Magazines and Other Publications

Business Week

http://www.businessweek.com/

In this online version of the popular business magazine are full-text articles, daily news, and content available only online—a standout site.

Notes:

_____

_____

_____

_____

_____

Chronicle of Higher Education

http://www.chronicle.merit.edu/

This education news site from the country's campuses features seven years of archived back issues. Categories: News, Academe Today (full text), Information Technology, Internet Resources, Events

Notes:

_____

_____

_____

_____

_____

Classroom Connect

http://www.classroom.net

From *Classroom Connect* magazine, this online site features a superb education-based search engine, a teachers' discussion forum, links to the best education-related Web sites, and a compendium of online schools—a very good site. Categories: Classroom Web, Materials for Educators, Teacher Contacts, Products, Links

Notes:

_____

_____

_____

_____

Creative Classroom Online

http://www.creativeclassroom.org/

The online version of *Creative Classroom* magazine, this site contains a teaching tips archive, downloadable units, and information about grants, prizes, and more.

Notes:

_____

_____

_____

_____

CyberSchool Magazine

http://www.cyberschoolmag.com

This is an excellent online magazine (attractive design, too). Visit the Electric Professor, monthly science features, and other featured articles that change monthly. The Surfin' Librarian features thousands of categorized links and online books.

Notes:

_____

_____

_____

_____

Education Week on the Web

http://www.edweek.org

One of the best education sites anywhere, it contains current and archived articles, research results, and news and views on education.

Notes:

_____

_____

_____

_____

Electronic Elementary Magazine: "The E-LINK"

http://www.inform.umd.edu/UMS+State/MDK12_Stuff/homepers/emag/

This magazine is a nonprofit, educational project that highlights interactive projects and creations of elementary grade students around the world.

Notes:

_____

_____

_____

_____

Electronic Learning

http://place.scholastic.com/el/index.htm

Find an abundance of information about technology in the classroom, including new and archived articles, grant information, and a lot more. Categories: Reports, News and Conferences, Grant Updates, Research Reports, Product Reviews, Emerging Technology

Notes:

_____

_____

_____

_____

Electronic School

http://www.electronic-school.com/

Published quarterly as a print and online supplement to *The American School Board Journal*, this is an excellent magazine site that provides full text articles and information for and about the wired school.

Notes:

_____

_____

_____

_____

Instructor Magazine

http://place.scholastic.com/instructor/index.htm

Serving elementary teachers nationwide, this Web site contains everything from strategies for integrating the curriculum and meeting the needs of the kids you teach to professional development opportunities and help with assessment.

Notes:

_____

_____

_____

_____

Mathematics Teacher

http://www.nctm.org/

Published by the National Council for Teachers of Mathematics, *Mathematics Teacher* is one of four online journals on the NCTM Web site. This journal offers some full articles but mostly abstracts.

Notes:

_____

_____

_____

_____

_____

National Geographic

http://www.nationalgeographic.com/main.html

An excellent online version of the magazine, this site offers long stories, beautiful pictures, and resources for both teachers and students.

Notes:

_____

_____

_____

_____

_____

Online Educator

http://www.ole.net/ole/

Get ready-to-use lesson plans and quick pointers on useful Internet resources that you and your students can access from your classroom.

Notes:

_____

_____

_____

_____

_____

Scientific American

http://www.sciam.com/index.html

An excellent online companion to the popular science magazine, this site has full-text-articles with colorful graphics and a searchable index of past articles.

Notes:

_____

_____

_____

_____

_____

Syllabus Magazine

http://www.sciam.com/index.html

Explore the use of technology in high schools and universities. Included are case studies, ten years of archived articles, and information on getting published by the magazine.

Notes:

Teacher Magazine

http://www.edweek.org/tm/tm.htm

Part of the Education Week on the Web site, *Teacher Magazine* is a slick, very informative online magazine. Changes are made weekly. Categories: Current Events, Research (policy and findings), Editorials, Features (full text)

Notes:

Teacher Talk

http://education.indiana.edu/cas/tt/tthmpg.html

Teacher Talk is published by the Center for Adolescent Studies at the School of Education, Indiana University, Bloomington, IN. It is a publication for preservice secondary education teachers.

Notes:

_____

_____

_____

_____

Teachers College Record

http://tcrecord.tc.columbia.edu/

The *Teachers College Record* is a journal of research, analysis, and commentary in the field of education. Articles are available as downloadable Adobe PDF files.

Notes:

_____

_____

_____

_____

Teacher's Edition Online (Teachnet.com)

http://www.teachnet.com/

A very good place for teachers to search for instruction ideas, the site also includes lesson plans, information on classroom management, humorous articles and anecdotes, and a lot more—a very extensive site. Categories: Teacher-2-Teacher, Lesson Ideas Resources & Links, How To, EdNews from the Web.

Notes:

_____

_____

_____

_____

Teaching Education

http://www.teachingeducation.com/

Devoted to teacher education at the undergraduate and graduate levels, *Teaching Education* Magazine's online version offers abstracts and full-text articles from the current print edition.

Notes:

_____

_____

_____

_____

Technological Horizons in Education (T.H.E.)

http://www.thejournal.com/

News on the world of computers and related technologies focuses on applications that improve teaching and learning for all ages. Categories: T.H.E. Forum, Events and Contests, Professional Development, Grants, Links

Notes:

_____

_____

_____

_____

TIME Magazine

http://pathfinder.com/@@@JzfugcAzLC3rSuk/time/

Part of the huge Pathfinder site, the online version of *Time* contains most of the printed articles from the weekly, as well as occasional Web specials.

Notes:

_____

_____

_____

_____

_____

U.S. News and World Report

http://www.usnews.com/usnews/main.htm

Another very good online version of a long-published news magazine, this site also features guides to colleges and graduate programs.

Notes:

_____

_____

_____

_____

_____

This Week's News

http://www.edweek.org/ew/current/thisweek.htm

This is an excellent site where you can find local, regional, and national educational issues making headlines today.

Notes:

_____

_____

_____

_____

_____

Mathematics

American Mathematical Society—eMath

http://e-math.ams.org/

The online home of the American Mathematical Society, this site offers information about the society, links to useful math-related places on the Web, and organization information.

Notes:

_____

_____

_____

_____

Amusing Mathematics Web Page

http://forum.swarthmore.edu/teachers/amusing.math.html

This is a good site that features frequently asked questions (and answers) about mathematics, as well as a canonical list of math jokes and jokes for math teachers.

Notes:

_____

_____

_____

_____

Appetizers and Lessons for Math and Reason

http://www.cam.org/~aselby/lesson.html

This useful site features activities teachers can use to introduce a mathematical concept or to fill up those last five minutes of the lesson when everything else has been done—many fine activities here.

Notes:

_____

_____

_____

_____

_____

Arithmetic Lesson Plans

http://forum.swarthmore.edu/arithmetic/arith.units.html

Very good lesson plans cover many different mathematical operations, including Montessori lessons and lessons using real world examples.

Notes:

_____

_____

_____

_____

_____

Ask Dr. Math

http://forum.swarthmore.edu/dr.math/

This very good site answers math questions you send in. The questions and answers are archived for searching and divided among elementary/middle school and high school/college/and beyond.

Notes:

_____

_____

_____

_____

Brain Teasers

http://www.eduplace.com/math/brain/

Divided among grades 3–4, 5–6, and 7 and above, these brainteasers can be used for lesson openers or to integrate math into other parts of the curriculum. One teaser is presented each week, though archived teasers are available.

Notes:

_____

_____

_____

_____

Busy Teachers—Math

http://www.ceismc.gatech.edu/busyt/math.html

From the Busy Teachers Web site comes links to other math lessons and ideas from around the Web. Categories: Fractals, Games and Toys, General, History, Lesson Plans/Classroom Activities.

Notes:

_____

_____

_____

_____

Dave's Math Tables

http://www.sisWeb.com/math/tables.htm

Featured are many math tables and tips on using them (check out the tip for remembering multiplying 9s!). Also, the entire site can be downloaded and printed out. Very cool! Categories: General Math, Algebra, Geometry, Trig, Odds and Ends, Statistics, Calculus

Notes:

_____

_____

_____

_____

Eisenhower National Clearinghouse for Mathematics and Science Education

http://www.enc.org/

Working to reform K–12 science and math education, the ENC site offers, among other things, free CD-ROMs (to schools) that feature the full text and graphics of the NCTM Curriculum and Evaluation Standards for School Mathematics and curriculum frameworks from several states.

Notes:

_____

_____

_____

Flash Cards for Kids

http://www.wwinfo.com/edu/flash.html

Online flash cards feature operations on addition, subtraction, multiplication, and division. You can select simple (only two numbers) or complex (up to 10 numbers), and numbers from 0–9, 0–99, or 0–999. It is fast-loading for questions and answers.

Notes:

_____

_____

_____

Fun With Numbers

http://www.newdream.net/~sage/old/numbers/

A good resource in its own way, this site features many things that you would not want to figure out on your own, including the first 28,915 odd primes, the first 999 factorials, and 1.2 million digits of pi.

Notes:

_____

_____

_____

_____

KnowZone

http://www.awl.com

The activities at this site can be utilized by students to help them improve their performance on standardized tests and aid in their work in the classroom.

Notes:

_____

_____

_____

_____

Math Education Resources

http://www.teleport.com/~vincer/math.html

This site offers links to many good online math sites. It lists lesson plans, curriculum guides, and interactive links, such as the Gallery of Interactive Geometry.

Notes:

_____

_____

_____

_____

Math Forum

http://forum.swarthmore.edu

In the search for math resources on the Web, this should be your first stop. This Swarthmore University site for teachers features math resources divided by subject and grade level, links to the best math sites on the Web, and the Dr. Math FAQ.

Notes:

_____

_____

_____

_____

Math Lesson Plans

http://ericir.syr.edu/Virtual/Lessons/Mathematics/index.html

There are many math lesson plans (text only) applicable to mostly grades K–8. Covered are problem solving, fractions, place value, and more.

Notes:

_____

_____

_____

_____

Mathematics

http://galaxy.einet.net/galaxy/Science/Mathematics.html

This search-engine-like site offers hundreds of links to math resources in many categories, which include academic organizations, articles, collections, directories, discussion groups, periodicals, and more.

Notes:

_____

_____

_____

_____

MathMagic Internet

http://forum.swarthmore.edu/mathmagic/

For teachers only, MathMagic is a K–12 telecommunications project. It provides strong motivation for students to use computer technology while increasing problem-solving strategies and communications skills. MathMagic posts challenges in each of four categories (K–3, 4–6, 7–9, and 10–12) to trigger each registered team to pair up with another team and engage in a problem-solving dialog. When an agreement has been reached, one solution is posted for every pair.

Notes:

_____

_____

_____

_____

National Council for Teachers of Mathematics

http://www.nctm.org

This site contains curriculum and education standards for mathematics, information on national math events, and links to other math-related sites.

Notes:

_____

_____

_____

_____

Topics in Mathematics

http://archives.math.utk.edu/topics/

This site is a repository for math links on the Web. Thousands of links are in well-defined categories.

Notes:

_____

_____

_____

_____

_____

_____

_____

_____

_____

_____

_____

_____

_____

_____

_____

_____

_____

_____

Public and Private Organizations

Academy for Educational Development

http://www.aed.org/

The Academy for Educational Development (AED) is an independent, nonprofit service organization committed to addressing human development needs in the United States and throughout the world.

Notes:

_____

_____

_____

_____

American Association of Physics Teachers

http://www.aapt.org/text.html

The American Association of Physics Teachers (AAPT) exists to enhance physics education for tomorrow's science professionals and to promote science literacy to the general public.

Notes:

_____

_____

_____

_____

American Association of School Administrators

http://www.aasa.org/

This is a very good AASA site with online papers, information about current educational news, and extensive organization information. Categories: News, Legislative Alerts, Job Postings, Membership Information, AASA Programs

Notes:

_____

_____

_____

_____

American Council on Education

http://www.acenet.edu./

The ACE seeks to advance the interests and goals of higher and adult education in a changing environment by providing leadership and advocacy on important issues, representing the views of the higher and adult education community to policy makers.

Notes:

_____

_____

_____

_____

American Educational Research Association

http://aera.net/

The American Educational Research Association is concerned with improving the educational process by encouraging scholarly inquiry related to education and by promoting the dissemination and practical application of research results.

Notes:

_____

_____

_____

_____

_____

American Educators Association

http://www.aeda.com/

The mission of American Educators Association is to utilize the Internet to provide an electronic information service for educators.

Notes:

_____

_____

_____

_____

_____

American Federation of Teachers
http://www.aft.org//index.htm

The Web site from the AFT features current union news, information about boycotts, and AFT press releases.

Notes:

_____

_____

_____

_____

_____

American Library Association
http://www.ala.org/

The American Library Association (ALA) is the oldest, largest, and one of the most influential library associations in the world.

Notes:

_____

_____

_____

_____

_____

American Literacy Council

http://www.under.org/alc/welcome.htm

The American Literacy Council provides resources and assistance to persons and organizations who are involved in the literacy crisis in America.

Notes:

_____

_____

_____

_____

_____

American Mathematical Society—eMath

http://e-math.ams.org/

The online home of the American Mathematical Society, this site offers information about the society, links to useful math-related places on the Web, and organization information.

Notes:

_____

_____

_____

_____

_____

American Montessori Education

http://www.amshq.org/

AMS is a nonprofit, non-discriminatory service organization dedicated to stimulating the use of the Montessori teaching approach in private and public schools.

Notes:

_____

_____

_____

_____

Americans for the Arts

http://www.artsusa.org/index.html

Americans for the Arts is the national membership organization for groups and individuals dedicated to advancing the arts and culture in communities across the United States.

Notes:

_____

_____

_____

_____

Association for Childhood Education International (ACEI)
http://www.udel.edu/bateman/acei/

ACEI is dedicated to the dual mission of promoting (1) the inherent rights, education and well-being of children from infancy through early adolescence, and (2) high standards of preparation and professional growth for educators.

Notes:

_____

_____

_____

_____

Association for Educational Communications and Technology
http://www.aect.org/

The mission of the Association for Educational Communications and Technology is to provide leadership by linking professionals holding a common interest in the use of educational technology and its application to the learning process.

Notes:

_____

_____

_____

_____

Association for Effective Schools

http://www.mes.org/

The Association for Effective Schools is a not-for-profit organization dedicated to developing and supporting the leadership and local capacity of schools, based on the processes of Effective Schools.

Notes:

_____

_____

_____

_____

Association for Supervision and Curriculum Development

http://www.ascd.org/

Founded in 1943, ASCD provides professional development in curriculum and supervision and initiates and supports activities to provide educational equity for all students.

Notes:

_____

_____

_____

_____

Association for the Advancement of Computing in Education

http://curry.edschool.virginia.edu/aace/

AACE (founded in 1981) is an international, educational, and professional organization dedicated to the advancement of the knowledge, theory, and quality of learning and teaching at all levels with information technology.

Notes:

_____

_____

_____

_____

_____

Benton Foundation

http://www.benton.org

Benton seeks to shape the emerging communications environment and to demonstrate the value of communications for solving social problems.

Notes:

_____

_____

_____

_____

_____

Best Practices in Education

http://www.bestpraceduc.org/

Best Practices in Education is a not-for-profit organization dedicated to working with American teachers to find effective educational practices from other countries to adapt and apply in United States schools.

Notes:

_____

_____

_____

_____

Center for Educational Reform

http://www.edreform.com

The Center for Educational Reform is a national, nonprofit education advocacy group and an active broker in providing resources, support and guidance for school reform to communities across the United States.

Notes:

_____

_____

_____

_____

Center for the Study of Professional Development

http://ed-Web3.educ.msu.edu/cspds/

The CSPD, based in MSU's College of Education, works with schools across Michigan. The college's collaboration with eight professional development schools focuses on bringing about change in the learning of educators at all levels, preservice teacher candidates, and children.

Notes:

_____

_____

_____

_____

CEO Forum on Education and Technology

http://www.ceoforum.org/

The CEO Forum on Education and Technology was founded in the fall of 1996 to help ensure that America's schools effectively prepare all students to be contributing citizens and productive workers in the 21st century.

Notes:

_____

_____

_____

_____

Computer 4 Kids

http://www.c4k.org/

Computers 4 Kids strives to provide equitable access to information and technology resources to students in our schools, homes, and communities.

Notes:

_____

_____

_____

_____

_____

Council for Exceptional Children

http://www.cec.sped.org/home.htm

The Council for Exceptional Children (CEC) is the largest international professional organization dedicated to improving educational outcomes for individuals with exceptionalities, students with disabilities, and/or the gifted.

Notes:

_____

_____

_____

_____

_____

Council of the Great City Schools

http://www.cgcs.org/

This site is maintained by an organization of the nation's largest urban public school systems, advocating K-12 education in inner-city schools, and governed by superintendents and board of education members from 50 cities across the country.

Notes:

_____

_____

_____

_____

Delta Kappa Gamma Society International

http://www.deltakappagamma.org/

The mission of the Delta Kappa Gamma Society International is to provide professional and personal growth for women educators and excellence in education.

Notes:

_____

_____

_____

_____

EdWeb: Exploring Technology and School Reform
http://edWeb.gsn.org/

With EdWeb, you can hunt down online educational resources around the world, learn about trends in education policy and information infrastructure development, examine success stories of computers in the classroom, and much, much more.

Notes:

_____

_____

_____

_____

Education Writers Association
http://www.ewa.org/

The Education Writers Association (EWA) is the national professional organization of education reporters.

Notes:

_____

_____

_____

_____

Educom

http://www.educom.edu/

Educom is a nonprofit consortium of higher education institutions that facilitates the introduction, use, and access to and management of information resources in teaching, learning, scholarship, and research.

Notes:

_____

_____

_____

_____

ERIC

http://www.indiana.edu/~eric_rec/index.html

A learning house on reading English and Communication, this site provides an abundance of useful information on everything from lesson plans to an extensive site on bibliographies. This one shouldn't be missed.

Notes:

_____

_____

_____

_____

I Have a Dream Foundation

http://www.ihad.org/

I Have a Dream is a comprehensive, long-term educational support program administered by the National I Have a Dream (IHAD) Foundation in New York.

Notes:

_____

_____

_____

_____

_____

International Literacy Institute

http://litserver.literacy.upenn.edu/ili/index.html

The mission of the ILI is to provide leadership in research, development, and training in the broad field of international literacy and development, with an emphasis on developing countries.

Notes:

_____

_____

_____

_____

_____

International Reading Association

http://www.ira.org

The International Reading Association seeks to promote high levels of literacy for all by improving the quality of reading instruction through studying the reading process and teaching techniques; serving as a clearinghouse for the dissemination of reading research through conferences, journals, and other publications; and actively encouraging the lifetime reading habit. Categories: Conferences & Conventions, Councils & Affiliates, Publications, International Projects, Research, Advocacy

Notes:

_____

_____

_____

International Society for Technology in Education

http://www.iste.org/

A nonprofit professional organization dedicated to the improvement of education through computer-based technology, it contains some archived articles and membership information.

Notes:

_____

_____

_____

International Technology Education Association

http://www.iteawww.org/

The International Technology Education Association (ITEA) is the largest professional educational association, principal voice, and information clearinghouse devoted to enhancing technology education through experiences in our schools (K–12).

Notes:

_____

_____

_____

_____

Library of Congress

http://marvel.loc.gov/

From the biggest library in the world comes perhaps one of the best Web sites ever. Search for legislative information, browse exhibits, or use their research search tool to search other Internet sites.

Notes:

_____

_____

_____

_____

MacArthur Foundation

http://www.macfdn.org/

The John D. and Catherine T. MacArthur Foundation is a private, independent grantmaking institution dedicated to helping groups and individuals foster lasting improvement in the human condition.

Notes:

_____

_____

_____

_____

Math/Science Nucleus Organization

http://www.msnucleus.org/

Math/Science Nucleus is a nonprofit (501(3)c), educational, and research organization composed of scientists, educators, and community members. It serves as a science resource center to assist school districts, teachers, and administrators.

Notes:

_____

_____

_____

_____

Michigan Electronic Library

http://mel.lib.mi.us/main-index.html

Though this site is mostly just links to other sites on the Web, the children's resource section has a lot of interesting content to review.

Notes:

_____

_____

_____

_____

_____

Microsoft's Education in Focus K–12

http://www.microsoft.com/education/k12/

A Microsoft site providing information about integrating technology with the classroom, it has some useful pages on Microsoft technology and a great deal on Windows 95 for schools.

Notes:

_____

_____

_____

_____

_____

Milken Family Foundation

http://www.mff.org/r_wnindex.html

The Milken Family Foundation's missions are to strengthen the profession of education by recognizing and rewarding outstanding educators; to expand their professional leadership and policy influence; and to encourage talented young people to become educators.

Notes:

_____

_____

_____

_____

NASA Education Resources

http://science.nas.nasa.gov/Services/Education/Resources/

From the National Aeronautic and Space Administration, this site includes educational resources for teachers, information on how to participate in NASA projects, and connections to other education servers.

Notes:

_____

_____

_____

_____

National Academy Foundation (NAF)

http://www.naf1.org/

The National Academy Foundation combines the knowledge and experience of leaders from education, business, and government to create programs that assist secondary school students in making the transition from school to work and/or college.

Notes:

_____

_____

_____

_____

National Academy of Child Development

http://www.nacd.org/

The National Academy for Child Development is an international organization of parents and professionals dedicated to helping children and adults reach their full potential.

Notes:

_____

_____

_____

_____

National Academy of Sciences

http://www2.nas.edu/nas/

The National Academy of Sciences is a private, nonprofit, self-perpetuating society of distinguished scholars engaged in scientific and engineering research, and dedicated to the furtherance of science and technology and to their use for the general welfare.

Notes:

_____

_____

_____

_____

National Art Education Association

http://www.naea-reston.org/

The NAEA's mission is to promote art education through professional development, service, advancement of knowledge, and leadership. NAEA is a nonprofit educational organization.

Notes:

_____

_____

_____

_____

National Assessment of Educational Progress

http://nces.ed.gov/naep/

The National Assessment of Educational Progress (NAEP) is mandated by Congress to monitor continuously the knowledge, skills, and performance of the nation's children and youth. Under this legislation, NAEP is required to provide objective data about student performance at national, regional, and, on a trial basis, state levels.

Notes:

_____

_____

_____

National Association for Gifted Children

http://www.nagc.org/

The National Association for Gifted Children (NAGC) is an organization of parents, educators, and other professionals and community leaders who unite to address the unique needs of children and youth with demonstrated gifts and talents as well as those children who may be able to develop their talent potential with appropriate educational experiences.

Notes:

_____

_____

_____

National Association for Multicultural Education

http://www.inform.umd.edu/CampusInfo/Committees/Assoc/NAME/

The National Association for Multicultural Education (NAME) was founded in 1991 to bring together professionals from all academic disciplines and from diverse educational institutions, organizations, and occupations who had an interest in multicultural education.

Notes:

_____

_____

_____

_____

National Association for Sport and Physical Education

http://www.aahperd.org/naspe/naspe.html

Across the country, more than 18,000 physical education, sport, fitness, and kinesiology professionals have teamed together to promote quality physical activity programs.

Notes:

_____

_____

_____

_____

National Association of Biology Teachers
http://www.nabt.org/

The National Association of Biology Teachers is the largest national association dedicated exclusively to the concerns of biology and life science educators.

Notes:

_____

_____

_____

_____

_____

National Association of Elementary School Principals
http://www.naesp.org/naesp.htm

The home page for the NAESP, this site offers information about the group, research projects, and membership information.

Notes:

_____

_____

_____

_____

National Association of Secondary School Principals

http://www.nassp.org/

NASSP's mission is to continue its commitment and support for principals, assistant principals, and other school leaders.

Notes:

_____

_____

_____

_____

_____

National Association of State Boards of Education

http://www.nasbe.org/

The National Association of State Boards of Education (NASBE) is a nonprofit, private association that represents state and territorial boards of education.

Notes:

_____

_____

_____

_____

_____

National Association of Students for Higher Education

http://nagps.varesearch.com/NASHE/nashe.html

NASHE was established in March 1995 to provide a national platform for student leaders to promote and defend the quality of higher education for all students in the United States.

Notes:

_____

_____

_____

_____

National Center for Research on Teacher Learning

http://ncrtl.msu.edu

Based in MSU's College of Education, the NCRTL has its emphasis on teacher learning and the center's desire to provide leadership in defining this new area of research.

Notes:

_____

_____

_____

_____

National Center for the Study of Writing and Literacy

http://www-gse.berkeley.edu/research/NCSWL/csw.homepage.html

The mission of the Center is to improve understanding of how writing is best learned and taught—from the early years through adulthood.

Notes:

_____

_____

_____

_____

National Center on Adult Literacy

http://litserver.literacy.upenn.edu/

The mission of NCAL is to (a) improve understanding of adult learners and their learning, (b) foster innovation and increase effectiveness in adult basic education and literacy work, and (c) expand access to information and build capacity for adult literacy service provision.

Notes:

_____

_____

_____

_____

National Center on Education and the Economy
http://www.ncee.org/

The National Center is organized to provide resources to schools, districts, and states interested in standards-based reform.

Notes:

_____

_____

_____

_____

National Center to Improve Practice in Special Education Through Technology, Media, and Materials (NCIP)
http://www.edc.org/FSC/NCIP/

The National Center to Improve Practice (NCIP) promotes the effective use of technology to enhance educational outcomes for students with sensory, cognitive, physical, and social/emotional disabilities. Categories: Art and Writing Connection, Video Profiles, NCIP Library

Notes:

_____

_____

_____

_____

National Council for History Education

http://www.history.org/nche/

The National Council for History Education is a nonprofit corporation dedicated to promoting the importance of history in schools and in society.

Notes:

_____

_____

_____

_____

_____

National Council for Teachers of Mathematics

http://www.nctm.org

This site contains curriculum and education standards for mathematics, information on national math events, and links to other math-related sites.

Notes:

_____

_____

_____

_____

_____

National Council for the Social Studies
http://www.ncss.org/home.html

This very deep site contains information about the NCSS, content for social studies educators, and membership information. It covers just about everything related to social studies curriculum. Check out the Notable Children's Trade Books.

Notes:

_____

_____

_____

_____

National Council of Teachers of English
http://www.ncte.org/

The National Council of Teachers of English, the world's largest subject-matter educational association, is devoted to improving the teaching of English and the language arts at all levels of education.

Notes:

_____

_____

_____

_____

National Dropout Prevention Center

http://www.dropoutprevention.org/

Located at Clemson University, the NDPC functions as a clearinghouse and research center as well as a provider of technical assistance. Its mission is to reduce America's dropout rate by meeting the needs of youth in at-risk situations.

Notes:

_____

_____

_____

_____

National Education Association (NEA)

http://www.nea.org/

The union of 2.3 million teachers has put together a very extensive Web site that contains union news, education and teacher briefs, and even some humor as well in the Recess section.

Notes:

_____

_____

_____

_____

National Educational Service

http://www.nes.org/

The National Educational Service works with educators and youth professionals to help foster environments in which all children will succeed.

Notes:

_____

_____

_____

_____

_____

National Endowment for the Arts

http://arts.endow.gov/

The National Endowment for the Arts is an independent agency of the federal government charged with supporting the arts in America for all Americans.

Notes:

_____

_____

_____

_____

_____

National Endowment for the Humanities

http://www.neh.fed.us/

A federal agency that supports learning in history, literature, philosophy, and other areas of the humanities, NEH funds research, education, museum exhibitions, documentaries, preservation, and activities in the states.

Notes:

_____

_____

_____

_____

_____

National Foundation for Gifted and Creative Children

http://www.nfgcc.org/

The main goal of this foundation is to get much needed information to the parents of gifted children.

Notes:

_____

_____

_____

_____

_____

National Foundation for the Improvement of Education
http://www.nfie.org/

NFIE provides grants and technical assistance to teachers, education support personnel, and higher education faculty and staff to improve student learning in the nation's public schools.

Notes:

_____

_____

_____

_____

National Institute for Literacy
http://novel.nifl.gov/

The National Institute for Literacy will execute the responsibilities enumerated in the National Literacy Act through the creation of system(s) which will enable every adult with literacy needs to receive services of the highest quality.

Notes:

_____

_____

_____

_____

National Middle School Association

http://www.nmsa.org/

The National Middle School Association (NMSA) serves as a voice for professionals, parents, and others interested in the educational and developmental needs of young adolescents (youth 10–15 years of age).

Notes:

_____

_____

_____

_____

_____

National Reading Conference

http://www.iusb.edu/~edud/EleEd/nrc/nrcindex.html

The National Reading Conference is a diverse group of literacy professionals drawn together by their interest in research.

Notes:

_____

_____

_____

_____

_____

National School Board Association

http://www.nsba.org/

NSBA is the nationwide advocacy and outreach organization for public school governance. Their Web site offers information about how they strive to foster equity and excellence in public elementary and secondary education in the United States through school board leadership.

Notes:

_____

_____

_____

_____

National Science Teachers Association

http://www.nsta.org/

The NSTA is the largest organization in the world committed to promoting excellence and innovation in science teaching and learning.

Notes:

_____

_____

_____

_____

Online Computer Library Center

http://www.oclc.org/

OCLC is a nonprofit, membership, library computer service and research organization dedicated to the public purposes of furthering access to the world's information and reducing information costs.

Notes:

_____

_____

_____

_____

_____

Parent Teacher Association (PTA)

http://www.pta.org/

The National PTA is the oldest and largest volunteer association in the United States working exclusively on behalf of children and youth.

Notes:

_____

_____

_____

_____

_____

Phi Delta Kappan

http://www.pdkintl.org/

Phi Delta Kappa is an international professional fraternity for men and women in education. The membership is composed of professionals in the field of education, graduate students preparing for careers in education, and undergraduates who are enrolled in or have successfully completed their student teaching.

Notes:

_____

_____

_____

_____

Project Appleseed

http://members.aol.com/pledgenow/appleseed/index.html

Project Appleseed is the not-for-profit national campaign advocating improvement in public schools by increasing and then organizing parental involvement in all 15,000 public school districts in the United States of America.

Notes:

_____

_____

_____

_____

Project Crossroads

http://www.rt66.com/~procross/

Project Crossroads is a not-for-profit educational resource organization which was founded in 1983 by a small group of educators who perceived that classroom teachers are greatly in need of good, relevant, and timely curricula to supplement the standard fare.

Notes:

_____

_____

_____

_____

Smithsonian Institution

http://www.si.edu/

Featured are links to What's New (exhibits), Perspectives, Activities, and Resources, which all provide information on a variety of subjects. A variety of graphics, sounds, and video are provided.

Notes:

_____

_____

_____

_____

Society for International Sister Schools

http://www.siss.org/

The Society for International Sister Schools (SISS) is an affiliation of schools of all levels linked throughout the world.

Notes:

_____

_____

_____

_____

_____

Teach for America

http://www.teachforamerica.org/

The national teacher corps is composed of outstanding recent college graduates of all academic majors and cultural backgrounds who commit two years to teach in under-resourced urban and rural public schools.

Notes:

_____

_____

_____

_____

_____

21st Century Teachers

http://www.21ct.org/

21st Century Teachers is a nationwide volunteer initiative encouraging 100,000 teachers to work with their colleagues to develop new skills for using technology in their teaching and learning activities.

Notes:

Research and Reference Resources

Alphabetical Listing of Colleges with Web Sites
http://www.uofdhigh.k12.mi.us/students/counsel/collaf.html

Just as the title says, this is a comprehensive list of colleges that have an online presence.

Notes:

_____

_____

_____

_____

Best of Our Knowledge
http://www.wamc.org/tbook/

The Best of Our Knowledge examines some of the issues unique to college campuses, looks at the latest research, and invites commentary from educational experts and college administrators. Shows are available as Real Audio broadcasts.

Notes:

_____

_____

_____

_____

BIG PAGE of Student Research Sites

http://www.mts.net/~jgreenco/student.html

This is a page of links divided by academic subject and is very functional.

Notes:

_____

_____

_____

_____

_____

CIA World Factbook

http://www.odci.gov/cia/publications/nsolo/wfb-all.htm

See your peace dividend at work. The CIA has put online an incredible resource for students and teachers (and anyone interested in other countries). From Afghanistan to Zimbabwe, and all countries in between, a wealth of facts is at your fingertips.

Notes:

_____

_____

_____

_____

_____

Citing Electronic Materials with the New MLA Guidelines

http://www-dept.usm.edu/~engdept/mla/rules.html

The new MLA guidelines describe how to cite references from electronic materials, such as Web sites or CD-ROMs.

Notes:

_____

_____

_____

_____

_____

College and University Home Pages

http://www.mit.edu:8001/people/cdemello/univ.html

This is an alphabetical list of over 3,000 colleges and universities, with links to their home pages.

Notes:

_____

_____

_____

_____

Disability Tables

http://Web.icdi.wvu.edu/disability/tables.html

The site contains many tables of demographic information about people with disabilities, such as working vs. non-working. Information is by state, for the U.S., and for the world.

Notes:

_____

_____

_____

_____

Digest of Education Statistics

http://nces.ed.gov/pubs/D96/index.html

This is the latest digest drawing from many sources, including the National Center for Education Statistics with many tables and figures comparing U.S. students to others around the world. This site also features many other publications available here: **http://nces.ed.gov/ncespub1.html**.

Notes:

_____

_____

_____

_____

EdWeb: Exploring Technology and School Reform

http://edWeb.gsn.org/

With EdWeb, you can hunt down online educational resources around the world, learn about trends in education policy and information infrastructure development, examine success stories of computers in the classroom, and much, much more.

Notes:

_____

_____

_____

_____

Education World Search Engine

http://www.education-world.com

This *Yahoo!*-like search engine is dedicated to educators and students. There are education news, chat forums, education site reviews, and links to commercial sites.

Notes:

_____

_____

_____

_____

Explorer Home Page

http://server2.greatlakes.k12.mi.us/

The Explorer is a network database system for contributing, organizing and delivering educational resources. Also, it contains lessons and resources dedicated to math and natural science.

Notes:

_____

_____

_____

_____

Impact of Technology

http://www.mcrel.org/connect/tech/impact.html

An excellent resource that features complete articles, surveys, etc., that explore the impact of technology in the classroom, this should be your first stop if you want to do research about technology and education.

Notes:

_____

_____

_____

_____

Internet Wiretap

http://wiretap.area.com/

This site features many online books, with authors like Mark Twain and Jane Austen. It also contains tons of government documents like international treaties and covenants, world constitutions, and U.S. government reports.

Notes:

_____

_____

_____

_____

Library of Congress

http://marvel.loc.gov/

From the biggest library in the world comes perhaps one of the best Web sites ever. Search for legislative information, browse exhibits, or use their research search tool to search other Internet sites.

Notes:

_____

_____

_____

_____

National Center for Education Statistics

http://www.ed.gov/

The National Center for Education Statistics fulfills a Congressional mandate to collect, collate, analyze, and report complete statistics on the condition of American education; conduct and publish reports; and review and report on education activities internationally.

Notes:

_____

_____

_____

_____

My Virtual Reference Desk

http://www.refdesk.com/

Links to U.S. and World newspapers, 200 search engines, 40 categories of encyclopedias, and much, much more are available here.

Notes:

_____

_____

_____

_____

Online Reference Works

http://www.cs.cmu.edu/references.html

From Central Michigan University, this is a growing list of Internet reference materials, including dictionaries, encyclopedias, and currency converters.

Notes:

_____

_____

_____

_____

_____

Roget's Thesaurus

http://www.thesaurus.com

This complete online searchable Roget's Thesaurus is perfect for finding the one special word.

Notes:

_____

_____

_____

_____

_____

Study Web

http://www.studyWeb.com/

This huge site with research and study resources nicely categorized is very good.

Notes:

_____

_____

_____

_____

_____

_____

Webster's Dictionary

http://work.ucsd.edu:5141/cgi-bin/http_webster

This searchable version of *Webster's Dictionary* has very detailed definitions.

Notes:

_____

_____

_____

_____

_____

_____

World-Wide Web Virtual Library

http://vlib.stanford.edu/Overview2.html

This very good site contains a categorical and exhaustive list of links on almost every subject.

Notes:

_____

_____

_____

_____

_____

_____

_____

_____

_____

_____

_____

_____

_____

_____

Science

AIMS Education Foundation

http://www.aimsedu.org/AIMS.html

AIMS Magazine offers teacher resources that focus on the "big ideas" in science. It also has a section to share your thoughts on science education with other teachers. Categories: Activity Archive, Idea Exchange, AIMS Magazine, Workshop Information, Downloads

Notes:

_____

_____

_____

_____

An Inquirer's Guide to the Universe

http://sln.fi.edu/planets/planets.html

Excellent site! It is devoted to space, science fact and fiction, and writing about space (students can post writings on the site). It also contains suggestions on how to use the guide in the classroom.

Notes:

_____

_____

_____

_____

Ask Dr. Science

http://www.ducksbreath.com/

Ask Dr. Science is a humorous, yet not quite scientific, site where Dr. Science answers your science questions, such as: Why doesn't a boiled egg turn vaporous?

Notes:

_____

_____

_____

_____

_____

Ask Science Questions

http://www-hpcc.astro.washington.edu/scied/sciask.html

This site provides links to other sites where you can send in questions to be answered by scientists. Included is everything from Ask an Antarctic Expert to Ask a Vocanologist.

Notes:

_____

_____

_____

_____

_____

Bill Nye, the Science Guy

http://nyelabs.kcts.org/

A good science site, if somewhat slow to load at times, features daily activities and information on the television show.

Notes:

_____

_____

_____

_____

_____

Dinsoauria

http://www.dinosauria.com/

This site features an excellent gallery of dinosaur images. The text is more suited for high school students, but elementary school students will love the pictures.

Notes:

_____

_____

_____

_____

Electronic Zoo

http://netvet.wustl.edu/e-zoo.htm

This is a huge repository of animal information. The Zoo is organized by animal, and clicking on an animal gives you a long list of links to related sites on the Web. Also featured are veterinary information and animal organization information.

Notes:

_____

_____

_____

_____

Exploratorium

http://www.exploratorium.edu/default.html

Another excellent science-based site, it has plenty of Science Explorer activities, including light and shadows and a virtual cow's eye dissection lesson. New activities are updated often. Categories: Events, Programs, Teacher Institute, Institute for Inquiry, Publications, Digital Library

Notes:

_____

_____

_____

_____

Franklin Institute Science Museum

http://sln.fi.edu/tfi/welcome.html

This is a beautiful site with many science resources. You can take virtual tours of many exhibits, check out units of study guides on living things and wind, and even pose a science question to an "expert."

Notes:

_____

_____

_____

_____

From Windmills to Whirligigs

http://www.sci.mus.mn.us/sln/vollis/

The Whirligig Farm is an in-depth exploration of science and art, concentrating on whirligigs, windmills and kinetic sculpture. It is lots of fun. Created by the Science Museum of Minnesota and their partner school, Museum Magnet School in St Paul, MN. Categories: Tour, Activities

Notes:

_____

_____

_____

_____

Galileo

http://www-hpcc.astro.washington.edu/scied/galileo.html

Galileo is a collection of scores of science lesson plans for K–12 science teachers for classroom use. Nicely divided by grade level, this site makes it very easy to find what you need and covers everything from animals to wind.

Notes:

_____

_____

_____

_____

Globe

http://www.globe.gov

Global Learning and Observations to Benefit the Environment (GLOBE) is a worldwide network of students, teachers, and scientists working together to study and understand the global environment. GLOBE students make a core set of environmental observations at or near their schools and report their data via the Internet—a very good site.

Notes:

_____

_____

_____

_____

Imagination Factory

http://users.hsonline.net/kidatart/

An excellent site devoted to recycling, The Imagination Factory includes lessons, activities, and links to other art and environmental sites on the Web. Categories: Creative, Education, Lessons/Activities, Links

Notes:

_____

_____

_____

_____

Interactive Frog Dissection

http://curry.edschool.virginia.edu/go/frog/

This is one of the most visited sites on the Web. Using multimedia and other technologies, students can virtually dissect a frog by following along with the step-by-step directions. The *Quick Time* videos do a good job of illustrating the process.

Notes:

_____

_____

_____

_____

JASON Project

http://www.jasonproject.org

A great site, it is one for all teachers! The JASON Foundation for Education, which was founded to administer the project, sponsors an annual scientific expedition which is the focus of an original curriculum developed for grades 4 through 8. During the expedition, students can take part in a live, interactive program. Categories: Past Expeditions, Newsroom, Press Kits

Notes:

_____

_____

_____

_____

MAD Scientist Network

http://medinfo.wustl.edu/~ysp/MSN/

Featuring science lessons, exhibits, and experiments, this site covers physics, biology, chemistry, and other areas. It is useful for teachers and students.

Notes:

_____

_____

_____

_____

Meteorology Guide

http://ww2010.atmos.uiuc.edu/(Gh)/guides/mtr/home.rxml

The Online Meteorology Guide is a collection of Web-based instructional modules that use multimedia technology and the dynamic capabilities of the Web—very comprehensive.

Notes:

_____

_____

_____

_____

_____

NASA K-12 Internet Initiative

http://quest.arc.nasa.gov:80/

NASA links to the current educational activities they are sponsoring and includes archived lessons, information about the initiative, and a lot more.

Notes:

_____

_____

_____

_____

_____

NASA Spacelink: An Aeronautics & Space Resource for Educators

http://spacelink.nasa.gov/.index.html

Another site from NASA, this one is devoted to space flight. It offers curriculum and instructional materials in math, history, geography, and language arts and also contains links to other aerospace resources.

Notes:

_____

_____

_____

_____

NASA - Teacher's Resource

http://imagers.gsfc.nasa.gov/

A very good resource provided by NASA, it provides lesson plans on remote sensing, biodiversity, and understanding light.

Notes:

_____

_____

_____

_____

National Science Education Standards

http://www.nap.edu/readingroom/books/nses/

Standards providing specific guidelines on content, teaching, professional development, assessment, science education programs, and systems are provided here.

Notes:

_____

_____

_____

_____

_____

National Science Foundation

http://www.nsf.gov/

Everything you need to know about the NSF is here.

Notes:

_____

_____

_____

_____

_____

National Wildlife Federation Animal Tracks

http://www.nwf.org/atracks/activity.html

A part of the National Wildlife Federation's Web site, Animal Tracks offers many lesson plans in five categories: Air, Habitat, People and the Environment, Wildlife and Endangered Species, and Water. Most pertain to grades K–8.

Notes:

_____

_____

_____

_____

Nine Planets

http://seds.lpl.arizona.edu/nineplanets/nineplanets/nineplanets.html

The Nine Planets is a multimedia tour of the solar system that includes information on more than just the nine planets with excellent images and lots of information.

Notes:

_____

_____

_____

_____

Possibilities in Science

http://kendaco.telebyte.com/billband/Possibilities.html

A site seeking to integrate the Internet into secondary science education, it features lesson plans, virtual field trips, and teacher discussion groups—one of the best technology-based teaching sites!

Notes:

_____

_____

_____

_____

Science Learning Network

http://www.sln.org/

Funded by the National Science Foundation, the Science Learning Network (SLN) is an online community of educators, students, schools, science museums, and other institutions demonstrating a new model for inquiry science education.

Notes:

_____

_____

_____

_____

Sea and Sky

http://www.seasky.org

This huge site devoted to astronomy and oceanography features image galleries, games, articles, and links to other like resources on the Web.

Notes:

_____

_____

_____

_____

Super Science Home Page

http://www.sci-ed-ga.org/modules/k6/ss/

This site is designed to encourage kids, teachers, and parents to do scientific experiments. It includes ideas for experiments, advice on performing and presenting experiments, an online contest, information on exciting books and multimedia titles, and information on applying for a new science grant for teachers.

Notes:

_____

_____

_____

_____

Virtual Pig Dissection

http://mail.fkchs.sad27.k12.me.us/fkchs/vpig/

This is definitely not as good as the Interactive Frog dissection, but it is still a useful alternative or enhancement to some biology classes that still do pig dissections.

Notes:

Volcano World

http://volcano.und.nodak.edu/

Here is information on every volcano in the world (at least, it seems like every one). You can view the volcanoes currently erupting and even check out short movies of eruptions. Each volcano is fully described. Also featured are resources for teachers.

Notes:

Why Ask Why

http://whyfiles.news.wisc.edu/

Find here a long list of questions (and answers) to life's little mysteries. It is a good place for kids to visit to learn something they have always wondered about and to get story ideas that are different and fun.

Notes:

_____

_____

_____

_____

_____

_____

_____

_____

_____

_____

_____

_____

_____

_____

_____

_____

_____

_____

Sites For Students

American Literacy Classics—A Chapter A Day

http://www.americanliterature.com

This site features online books such as *The Wizard of Oz*, *Moby Dick*, and *The Red Badge of Courage*. It is set up so that you can read a chapter a day. (Be warned, though, *Moby Dick* is 135 chapters long!)

Notes:

Animals Myths and Legends

http://www.ozemail.com.au/~oban/

Oban the Knowledge Keeper and his fellow storytellers take you through the world of myths and legends. Learn the importance of these stories to the Aboriginal peoples of Australia and other cultures. Story pages fit nicely on the screen and include some illustrations. At the playroom you'll find coloring pages and a crossword.

Notes:

Bill Nye, the Science Guy

http://nyelabs.kcts.org/

A good science site, it is somewhat slow to load at times and features daily
activities and information on the television show.

Notes:

_____

_____

_____

_____

Challenge Zone

http://208.132.221.18/asd/edconn/chzone/zone2.htm

This is an excellent site that provides an exciting environment for learning that
includes exploring the Internet with your students. Interesting challenges focusing
on important topics in all subject areas appear weekly and are organized into four-
to six-week themes.

Notes:

_____

_____

_____

_____

Cool Word of the Day

http://130.63.218.180/~wotd/

Nobody said literacy couldn't be attained one word at a time. This site has, as the title says, a "cool" feature word of the day and also accepts submissions.

Notes:

_____

_____

_____

_____

_____

Create Your Own Newspaper

http://crayon.net/

A free site, CRAYON lets kids (and adults) create their very own newspapers. With downloadable links to real newspaper and broadcast stories and graphics, this is a great site to use to experiment and learn the ins and out of journalism.

Notes:

_____

_____

_____

_____

_____

CyberKids Home

http://www.cyberkids.com

This is a site designed for younger kids to publish their artwork, writing, and even music (in midi format, only). This is a very highly regarded site, one of the first, and still one of the best. Categories: Contests, Gallery, Games and Puzzles, Reading Room, Young Composers

Notes:

_____

_____

_____

_____

CyberSeuss

http://www.afn.org/~afn15301/drseuss. html

The home page of Dr. Seuss discusses everything about his life and work. As far as I can tell, none of the books are online (at least, none are authorized to be online). Still, there are some useful things here, and it's just interesting to read about the man who created the Lorax, Horton, and the Cat in the Hat.

Notes:

_____

_____

_____

_____

Dinosauria

http://www.dinosauria.com/

This site features an excellent gallery of dinosaur images. The text is more suited for high school students, but elementary school students will love the pictures.

Notes:

_____

_____

_____

_____

_____

Disney's Storybooks

http://www.disney.com/DisneyBooks/new/StoryBook/StoryBook.html

Read Disney's "improved" serialized storybooks online—now featuring *The Hunchback of Notre Dame* and *Aladdin*. Each story includes big pictures and easy-to-read text.

Notes:

_____

_____

_____

_____

_____

4kids Treehouse

http://www.4kids.com/

This is an excellent site that features links to other popular places on the Web in the following categories: reading, science, social studies, entertainment, playroom, and projects. The reading and social studies sections are standouts.

Notes:

Global Show-n-Tell Home Page

http://www.telenaut.com/gst/

Literacy isn't just reading and writing. Artwork, too, is a method of displaying your knowledge and appreciating the insights of others. This page lets children show their work to kids around the world and includes many links to children's art works on the Web.

Notes:

Flash Cards for Kids

http://www.wwinfo.com/edu/flash.html

Online flash cards feature operations on addition, subtraction, multiplication, and division. You can select simple (only two numbers) or complex (up to 10 numbers), and numbers from 0–9, 0–99, or 0–999. Fast-loading for questions and answers.

Notes:

_____

_____

_____

_____

Grimm's Fairy Tales

gopher://ftp.std.com/11/obi/book/Fairy.Tales/Grimm

A very bare-bones site with no pictures, it does have over 40 fairy tales that deserve rereading every so often. Complete text is available.

Notes:

_____

_____

_____

_____

How Things Work

http://www.phys.virginia.edu/Education/Teaching/HowThingsWork/

From the author of a physics book on how everyday things works, this site features questions and answers about (obviously) how things work.

Notes:

_____

_____

_____

_____

_____

Internet Public Library Story Hour

http://www.ipl.org/youth/StoryHour/

Need a story to read? This site at the University of Michigan offers full-length stories with pictures. The last I checked, they had *The Tortoise and the Hare* by Rebeccah J. Kamp and a few others.

Notes:

_____

_____

_____

_____

_____

Kid Pub

http://www.kidpub.org/kidpub/

Another place for kids to publish their stories on the Web. Very cool site. Categories: Publish Your Story, KidPub Schools, Publisher's Picks.

Notes:

_____

_____

_____

_____

Kids Com

http://www.kidscom.com/orakc/index2.shtml

This is a great place for kids to explore the Internet and interact with electronic pals. Games and arts and crafts are provided. Users must register (free) to view the entire site. There is a section for teachers, too. Categories: Around the World, Make New Friends, Kids Talk, Just for Fun, Parents and Teachers

Notes:

_____

_____

_____

_____

Kids Space

http://www.kids-space.org/

Another site featuring kids' artwork, this one features the art of children done in English and Japanese. They will accept submissions of stories and art work from children. Categories: Story Book, Kids Gallery, Beanstalk

Notes:

National Wildlife Federation Just for Kids

http://www.nwf.org/nwf/kids/

This site features four different games and tours of water, wetlands, endangered species, and public lands. Kids can explore the outdoors through activity lessons posted on the site.

Notes:

Students Can Learn on Their Own

http://www.erols.com/interlac/

This site provides information and resources for the independent student, including a large list of published materials.

Notes:

_____

_____

_____

_____

_____

Virtual Frog Dissection Kit Version 2

http://george.lbl.gov/dissect.html

One of the most popular sites on the Web, this one lets you virtually dissect a frog. Very cool! The site is slow at times but well worth the wait.

Notes:

_____

_____

_____

_____

_____

Wacky Web Tales

http://www.eduplace.com/tales/

This site is a great grammar teacher. Students fill out an online form and, based upon their word choices, create Wacky Web Tales. Geared more towards upper elementary students (4th grade and up), it is kind of like the old Mad Libs books.

Notes:

_____

_____

_____

_____

Why Ask Why

http://whyfiles.news.wisc.edu/

A long list of questions (and answers) to life's little mysteries, the site is a good place for kids to visit to learn something they have always wondered about and to get story ideas that are different and fun.

Notes:

_____

_____

_____

_____

Yahooligans! The Web Guide for Kids

http://www.yahooligans.com/

This is a *Yahoo!* search engine for kids featuring the sites in which they may be most interested. Categories: Around the World, Art Soup, Computers and Games, Entertainment, School Bell, Science & Oddities, Sports & Recreation, The Scoop

Notes:

_____

_____

_____

_____

_____

_____

_____

_____

_____

_____

_____

_____

_____

_____

_____

_____

Social Studies and History

1492: An Ongoing Voyage

http://sunsite.unc.edu/expo/1492.exhibit/Intro.html

From the Library of Congress, this site is a feature-packed enriching lesson on the voyage of Columbus and the impacts of the discovery of the New World. It offers maps and other historical documents.

Notes:

_____

_____

_____

_____

America's Life Histories—Manuscripts from the Federal Writer's Project

http://lcWeb2.loc.gov/ammem/wpaintro/wpahome.html

The Federal Writer's Project was a Depression-era government plan that put writers to work chronicling the history of the country in the words of those who lived through it. This site contains thousands of interviews done for this project.

Notes:

_____

_____

_____

_____

Atlapedia Online

http://www.atlapedia.com/index.html

Atlapedia Online contains key information on every country of the world. Each country profile provides facts and data on geography, climate, people, religion, language, history and economy, making it ideal for personal or family education and students of all ages.

Notes:

_____

_____

_____

_____

Core Documents of U.S. Democracy

http://www.access.gpo.gov/su_docs/dpos/coredocs.html

They're all here, from the Bill of Rights to the Declaration of Independence, complete and with narrative text explaining their importance and nuances. Categories: Legislative and Legal, Regulatory, Office of the President, Demographic, Economic, and Miscellaneous

Notes:

_____

_____

_____

_____

Eyewitness—History Through the Eyes of Those Who Lived It
http://www.ibiscom.com/index.html

Using diaries, interviews, newspaper stories, and other first-hand sources, this site recounts historical events such as Custer's Last Stand and the Great San Francisco Earthquake.

Notes:

_____

_____

_____

_____

_____

First Nations Histories

http://dickshovel.netgate.net/Compacts.html

A geographic overview of more than 40 Native American nations, the site is very detailed, and even though it lacks many graphics, this is an excellent resource.

Notes:

_____

_____

_____

_____

_____

Flints and Stones—Life in Prehistory

http://www.ncl.ac.uk/~nantiq/menu.html

An excellent site that takes you on a tour of life in prehistoric times, this site blows away the myths and legends surrounding prehistory and manages to be educational and interesting at the same time. No Fred or Wilma here!

Notes:

_____

_____

_____

_____

_____

Historical Text Archive

http://www.msstate.edu/Archives/History/index.html

Here's some good reading. This site provides historical texts from the United States and other countries. It also has many links to other history sites.

Notes:

_____

_____

_____

_____

_____

History Channel

http://www.historychannel.com/

This excellent site features special history events. Check out the Real Audio collection of historic sound clips and speeches. Also, don't miss This Day in History, which lets you search for the events that happened on any day of the year.

Notes:

_____

_____

_____

History/Social Studies Web Site for K–12 Teachers

http://www.execpc.com/~dboals/boals.html

This huge (we're talking unbelievably big) catalog site is full of history and social studies resources for teachers. Categories: Archaeology, Creative Applications, Diversity, Electronic Texts, Genealogy, General Guides, Geography, Economics, Government, American History, European History, Non-Western History Sites, General History, Humanities, Resources for Writers, Resources for Parents

Notes:

_____

_____

_____

H-Net, Humanities & Social Sciences Online

http://h-net2.msu.edu/

A huge site from Michigan State University dedicated to the humanities. this site also contains the online companion to *Liberty*, the PBS series on the American Revolution, and many e-mail discussion lists on the humanities.

Notes:

_____

_____

_____

_____

HyperHistory

http://www.hyperhistory.com/online_n2/History_n2/a.html

This site contains time lines with links to stories on major world events. Based on the synchronoptic concept and functions as a companion to the seminal World History Chart—a very effective resource for all students and teachers.

Notes:

_____

_____

_____

_____

Martin Luther King, Jr.

http://www.seattletimes.com/mlk/index.html

From the *Seattle Times*, this in-depth look at the life and impact of Martin Luther King, Jr. is full of details and descriptions. It includes sound clips of the "I Have a Dream" and "Promised Land" speeches—a very good site.

Notes:

_____

_____

_____

_____

Matewan

http://www.matewan.com/

One of the most famous small towns in America, Matewan was the site of bloody coal mine wars and wars of another kind (the infamous Hatfield and McCoy feud). The town proves proud of its history by providing information about both, as well as links for more information.

Notes:

_____

_____

_____

_____

Middle Ages

http://www.burbank.k12.ca.us/~luther/midages/beginhere.html

Created by seventh grade students to teach about the Middle Ages, this site is included here not only for its content, which is good, but also because it serves as a good example as one of the ways teachers can integrate the Internet in the curriculum. It includes a good set of online resources, too.

Notes:

_____

_____

_____

_____

Slave Voices

http://odyssey.lib.duke.edu/slavery/

From the Special Collections Library of Duke University, the story of slavery is retold with the documents of the period. Bills of sale, newspaper advertisements, diaries, etc. are reproduced and interpreted. This is a very good site.

Notes:

_____

_____

_____

_____

Social Studies Lesson Plans and Resources

http://www.csun.edu/~hcedu013/

Over 100 social studies lesson plans are provided by Dr. Marty Levine, Professor of Secondary Education, California State University, Northridge (CSUN) It is a very good set of resources. Categories: Lesson Plans and Teaching Strategies, Online Activities, Teaching Current Events

Notes:

_____

_____

_____

_____

Social Studies Projects

http://www.eduplace.com/projects/ssproj.html

This site serves as an exchange for educators to collaborate on many online social studies projects. It includes lesson plans and ideas on weather, geography, and more.

Notes:

_____

_____

_____

_____

Today Page (This Day in History)

http://www.uta.fi/~blarku/today.html

This is a site that highlights what happened this day in history in countries all over the world and also has information on what is happening in the near future.

Notes:

_____

_____

_____

_____

United Nations Development Program

http://www.undp.org/

The United Nations Development Program extends to 174 countries and territories, working to eliminate poverty and regenerate the environment and for job creation and the advancement of women. Categories: Focus Areas, UN System, News, Publications, Statistics

Notes:

_____

_____

_____

_____

U.S. Historical Documents

http://www.law.uoknor.edu/ushist.html

From the Magna Carta to President Clinton's second inaugural address and everything in between, this site has the historical record of the United States in hypertext format. Very nice!

Notes:

_____

_____

_____

_____

World of Benjamin Franklin

http://sln.fi.edu/franklin/rotten.html

A "virtual" book on Benjamin Franklin, it is included in this guide not so much because of its content, which is outstanding, but because it serves as an example of what a class can post on the Web as a group.

Notes:

_____

_____

_____

_____

World's Greatest Speeches

http://www.audionet.com/speeches/

This site contains excerpts (and full versions) of many of the greatest speeches ever recorded. You will need a Real Audio player (free) to hear them.

Notes:

_____

_____

_____

_____

_____

_____

_____

_____

_____

_____

_____

_____

_____

_____

_____

_____

_____

_____

Special Education

Asperger's Disorder/Autism

Asperger's Disorder Home Page

http://www.ummed.edu/pub/o/ozbayrak/asperger.html

This site by Dr. Kaan Ozbayrak provides a good informative overview of the disorder, and it provides links to other related sites, as well as a list of doctors who evaluate individuals with Asperger's Disorder.

Notes:

_____

_____

_____

_____

Asperger's Syndrome

http://www.wpi.edu/~trek/aspergers.html

Part of a personal home page, this site contains information about Asperger's Syndrome and links to other related sites on the Web.

Notes:

_____

_____

_____

_____

Asperger's Syndrome Support Network

http://www.vicnet.net.au/vicnet/community/asperger.htm

This is an Australian site that is very detailed, heavy on content, and extremely informative.

Notes:

_____

_____

_____

_____

_____

Autism Society of America

http://www.autism-society.org/

ASA is dedicated to increasing public awareness about autism and the day-to-day issues faced by individuals with autism, their families, and the professionals with whom they interact.

Notes:

_____

_____

_____

_____

_____

Center for the Study of Autism

http://www.autism.org/

The Center provides information about autism to parents and professionals and conducts research on the efficacy of various therapeutic interventions.

Notes:

_____

_____

_____

_____

_____

Online Asperger's Syndrome Information and Support

http://www.udel.edu/bkirby/asperger/

This very comprehensive site is dedicated to Asperger's Syndrome, with many links and lots of content.

Notes:

_____

_____

_____

_____

_____

Society for the Autistically Handicapped

http://www.rmplc.co.uk/eduweb/sites/autism/index.html

This UK site provides a significant amount of information on Autism, including breaking news, facts about autism, and treatment news.

Notes:

_____

_____

_____

_____

_____

_____

_____

_____

_____

_____

_____

_____

_____

_____

_____

_____

_____

_____

Assistive Technology

Assistive Technology Adaptive Computing Software Project

http://www.wildmantim.com/acsp/

Their stated mission is to serve and supply individual consumers and educational institutions with low cost, reliable software and hardware solutions available through the Internet.

Notes:

_____

_____

_____

Alliance for Technology Access

http://www.ataccess.org/

The Alliance for Technology Access (ATA) is a network of community-based resource centers dedicated to providing information and support services to children and adults with disabilities and increasing their use of standard, assistive, and information technologies.

Notes:

_____

_____

_____

Assistive Technology Web Report

http://projects.iat.unc.edu/atwr/

This online guide to assistive technology features an annotated list of Internet resources and reports that deal with assistive technology.

Notes:

_____

_____

_____

_____

Basic Skills in Assistive Technology

http://pursuit.rehab.uiuc.edu/pursuit/dis-resources/assistive-tech/basic-skills/basic-skills.html

The purpose of this training program is to provide a broad overview which begins to address the information needs of consumers and professionals alike. This lesson is downloadable.

Notes:

_____

_____

_____

_____

Center for Applied Special Technology
http://www.cast.org/

CAST (Center for Applied Special Technology) is a not-for-profit organization whose mission is to expand opportunities for individuals with disabilities through innovative computer technology.

Notes:

_____

_____

_____

_____

Equal Access to Software and Information
http://www.rit.edu/~easi/

EASI's mission is to serve as a resource to the education community by providing information and guidance in the area of access-to-information technologies by individuals with disabilities.

Notes:

_____

_____

_____

_____

Mac Access Passport Online

http://17.254.3.40/MAP/IntroMAP

The Mac Access Passport database lists those hard-to-find products that help people with disabilities use a Macintosh computer. It includes information on more than 100 software and hardware tools.

Notes:

Virtual Assistive Technology Center

http://www.sped.ukans.edu/~dlance/atech.html

This site features free assistive technology software and links to other assistive technology sites.

Notes:

Attention Deficit Disorder

50 Tips on Classroom Management for ADD
http://www.chadd.org/50class.htm

This well-written and easy-to-read paper details strategies teachers can use to manage the classroom effectively for students with ADD.

Notes:

_____

_____

_____

_____

_____

Attention Deficit Disorder
http://www.ns.net/users/BrandiV/

This site is dedicated to ADD/ADHD and related issues.

Notes:

_____

_____

_____

_____

_____

Attention Deficit Disorder Frequently Asked Questions

http://www.bubbaonline.com

This is a very informative FAQ about Attention Deficit Disorder.

Notes:

_____

_____

_____

_____

_____

_____

_____

Attention Deficit Disorder WWW Archive

http://www.realtime.net/cyanosis/add/

Find here an archive site, with papers etc., dedicated to ADD.

Notes:

_____

_____

_____

_____

_____

_____

Attention Deficit Disorders, Hyperactivity & Associated Disorders

http://www.execpc.com/~calliope/

This book describes the disorders and their possible causes, as well as recognizing what ADD is not. It also provides parents, educators and health professionals with knowledge to enable them to effectively help children with ADD and related disorders.

Notes:

_____

_____

_____

_____

Classroom Management of Attention Deficits

http://www.Webcom.com/rusleepy/articles/101tips.html

At this site are 101 tips (102, actually) explaining the techniques teachers can utilize when teaching students with attention deficit disorder.

Notes:

_____

_____

_____

_____

One ADD Place

http://www.greatconnect.com/oneaddplace/

This "virtual neighborhood" consolidates in one place information and resources relating to Attention Deficit Disorder (A.D.D.), ADIHD, and Learning Disorders (LD). Categories: Treasure Chest, Products, Library, Calendar, Professional Services

Notes:

_____

_____

_____

_____

WWW Attention Deficit Disorder FAQ

http://www3.sympatico.ca/frankk/

Here is an Internet FAQ for parents and teachers of ADD-diagnosed children interested in ADD.

Notes:

_____

_____

_____

_____

Clearinghouses

ASKERIC Home Page

http://ericir.syr.edu/

ERIC is the Educational Resources Information Center (ERIC), a federally funded national information system that provides, through its 16 subject-specific clearinghouses, associated adjunct clearinghouses, and support components, a variety of services and products on a broad range of education-related issues.

Notes:

_____

_____

_____

_____

Disability Related Sites on the WWW

http://thearc.org/misc/dislnkin.html

Hundreds of links to other disability-related sites are organized by category.

Notes:

_____

_____

_____

_____

Internet Resources for Special Children (IRSC)

http://www.irsc.org/

The IRSC Web site is dedicated to communicating information relating to the needs of children with disabilities on a global basis.

Notes:

_____

_____

_____

_____

_____

National Clearinghouse of Rehabilitation Training Materials

http://www.nchrtm.okstate.edu/index.html

The Clearinghouse is funded by a grant from the Rehabilitation Services Administration in the U.S. Department of Education and is its sole clearinghouse.

Notes:

_____

_____

_____

_____

_____

Special Education Resource on the Internet (SERI)

http://www.hood.edu/seri/serihome.htm

The site has a huge collection of special education links in many different categories—so many links, in fact, that it is a little difficult to find what you are looking for. It is still useful, though.

Notes:

_____

_____

_____

_____

_____

Teacher's Guide to U.S.D.O.E. Clearinghouses

http://www.ed.gov/pubs/TeachersGuide/clearing.html

This is a guide to the ERIC clearinghouses provided by the U.S. Department of Education.

Notes:

_____

_____

_____

_____

_____

Disability Research and Resources

Council for Disability Rights

http://www.disabilityrights.org

A nonprofit organization, the CDR provides public education, information, referrals, counseling, job training, and many other services to the disabled community. Categories include national and local news, an ADD FAQ for non-lawyers, and frequently asked questions about protecting personal rights.

Notes:

_____

_____

_____

_____

Disability Related Resources on the Web

http://thearc.org/misc/dislnkin.html

This site has many links to disability-related sites.

Notes:

_____

_____

_____

_____

National Clearinghouse of Rehabilitation Training Materials
http://www.nchrtm.okstate.edu/index.html

The NCRTM's Web site includes information on recent publications, videos and other rehabilitation training materials, downloadable documents, links to other rehabilitation information sources, and information about materials available from the NCRTM by mail.

Notes:

_____

_____

_____

_____

_____

_____

_____

_____

_____

_____

_____

_____

_____

_____

_____

_____

_____

Down Syndrome

Down Syndrome Resource League

http://www.qtm.net/~mtedesco/dsrl_home.htm

The Down Syndrome Resource League is a local (SW Michigan) organization of families and interested persons working to improve opportunities for those touched by Down syndrome.

Notes:

_____

_____

_____

_____

Down Syndrome WWW Page

http://www.nas.com/downsyn/

This site contains information about Down syndrome, including a FAQ.

Notes:

_____

_____

_____

_____

National Association for Down Syndrome

http://www.nads.org/

NADS, a not-for-profit organization, was founded in Chicago in 1961 by parents of children with Down syndrome who felt a need to create a better environment and bring about understanding and acceptance of people with Down syndrome.

Notes:

National Down Syndrome Society

http://www.ndss.org/

The National Down Syndrome Society was established in 1979 to increase public awareness about Down syndrome to assist families in addressing the needs of children born with this genetic condition, and to sponsor and encourage scientific research—a very good Web site.

Notes:

Dyslexia

Dyslexia 2000

http://www.futurenet.co.uk/charity/ado/index.html

Containing copius information about dyslexia including first-hand reports and many essays and articles, this site also contains lots of information about dyslexia-related software, other WWW sites, and advice and information for people with dyslexia. This very good site is not updated very often.

Notes:

_____

_____

_____

_____

Dyslexia Archive

http://129.12.200.129/dyslexia/www/archive.html

This site has information about dyslexia, including information about appropriate software and groups dedicated to dyslexia.

Notes:

_____

_____

_____

_____

Dyslexia Center

http://www.dyslexiacenter.com/

This site features some content on dyslexia written by students of the Dyslexia Center. The Center offers informational workshops, assessments, and tutorial services.

Notes:

_____

_____

_____

_____

_____

Dyslexia—The Gift

http://www.dyslexia.com/

A forum for networking and sharing information about creative thinking, dyslexia, and other learning differences is at this site.

Notes:

_____

_____

_____

_____

_____

International Dyslexia Association

http://www.interdys.org/

The International Dyslexia Association is an international, 501C(3) nonprofit, scientific and educational organization dedicated to the study and treatment of dyslexia. Categories: Conferences, Information, Branch Services, Technology, Research, Bulletin Board

Notes:

_____

_____

_____

_____

_____

_____

_____

_____

_____

_____

_____

_____

_____

_____

_____

Emotional Impairment

American Academy of Child and Adolescent Psychology
http://www.aacap.org

The AACAP's Web site includes 52 Facts for Families, guides for families confronting behavior problems. Categories: Breaking News, Facts for Families, Journals and Publications, Research and Training

Notes:

_____

_____

_____

_____

Arc

http://thearc.org/welcome.html

The Arc claims to be the country's largest voluntary organization committed to the welfare of all children and adults with mental retardation and their families.

Notes:

_____

_____

_____

_____

Emotional Impairment Frequently Asked Questions

http://www.bubbaonline.com

A very informative FAQ about emotional impairments is the content of this site.

Notes:

_____

_____

_____

_____

_____

_____

_____

_____

_____

_____

_____

_____

_____

_____

_____

_____

_____

_____

_____

_____

General

Band-Aids and Blackboards

http://funrsc.fairfield.edu/~jfleitas/contents.html

This is a site dedicated to sensitizing children to what it's like to grow up with a medical problem. Categories: Information for Kids, Teens, and Adults

Notes:

_____

_____

_____

_____

Classroom Management Special Education

http://www.pacificnet.net/~mandel/SpecialEducation.html

Here are many suggestions from practicing teachers (from the Teachers Helping Teachers site) detailing different methods of classroom management and how to implement them (applicable to all grades).

Notes:

_____

_____

_____

_____

Council for Exceptional Children

http://www.cec.sped.org/

The Council for Exceptional Children (CEC) is the largest international professional organization dedicated to improving educational outcomes for individuals with exceptionalities, students with disabilities, and/or the gifted.

Notes:

_____

_____

_____

_____

_____

Disability.com

http://disability.com/

A commercial site, a little heavy on the advertising, offers current news to people with disabilities and features a heavily used reader exchange.

Notes:

_____

_____

_____

_____

_____

Disability Tables

http://Web.icdi.wvu.edu/disability/tables.html

This site contains many tables of demographic information about people with disabilities, such as working vs. non-working and information by state, for the U.S., and for the world.

Notes:

_____

_____

_____

_____

Intervention Techniques

http://curry.edschool.virginia.edu/go/cise/ose/information/interventions.html

This site features effective teaching techniques for special education students. The techniques are abstracted for easy reviewing and include subjects such as reading, behavioral problems, and content instruction.

Notes:

_____

_____

_____

_____

National Information Center for Children and Youth with Disabilities

http://www.nichcy.org/

NICHCY is the national information and referral center that provides information on disabilities and disability-related issues for families, educators, and other professionals. Their focus is children and youth (birth to age 22).

Notes:

_____

_____

_____

_____

_____

_____

_____

_____

_____

_____

_____

_____

_____

_____

_____

_____

_____

Hearing Impairment

Animated American Sign Language Dictionary

http://www.feist.com/~randys/

A very cool site, it has just what the title implies: animated pictures (with captions) that show how to sign words. Impressive!

Notes:

_____

_____

_____

_____

Council on Education of the Deaf

http://www.educ.kent.edu/deafed/

The purpose of this Internet site is to facilitate the identification and sharing of information; find questions and collaborative opportunities concerning the education of deaf/hard-of-hearing students.

Notes:

_____

_____

_____

_____

Deaf Magazine

http://www.deaf-magazine.Org/

Archived issues of *Deaf Magazine* are available here.

Notes:

_____

_____

_____

_____

_____

Deaf Resource Library

http://www.deaflibrary.org

This is an online collection of reference material and links intended to educate and inform people about deaf cultures in Japan and the United States, as well as deaf and hard-of-hearing related topics.

Notes:

_____

_____

_____

_____

Deaf World Web

http://dww.deafworldweb.org/

Advertised as the largest and leading multipurpose deaf-related Web site, it provides information on all subjects from socio-cultural resources to references around the world.

Notes:

_____

_____

_____

_____

_____

Gallaudet University

http://www.gallaudet.edu/

The world's only four-year university for deaf and hard-of-hearing undergraduate students maintains this site.

Notes:

_____

_____

_____

_____

_____

Laws, Standards, and IEPs

Americans with Disabilities Act

http://www.bubbaonline.com

You can find here the full text of the Americans with Disabilities Act.

Notes:

_____

_____

_____

_____

_____

Appendix C—Notice of Interpretation

http://www.escambia.k12.us/adminoff/ese/Law/IDEAreg/rinterp.htm

Find the complete text of Notice of Interpretation.

Notes:

_____

_____

_____

_____

_____

IDEA

http://www.edlaw.net/public/contents.htm

The complete IDEA text is at this site.

Notes:

_____

_____

_____

_____

_____

IEP Interpretation (Questions and Answers on IEPs)

http://www.bubbaonline.com

An easy-to-read document is presented in a question-and-answer format that explains IEPs, their implementation, and the precedents and standards affecting their implementation.

Notes:

_____

_____

_____

_____

_____

Individualized Education Program: A Road Map to Success

http://www.hyperlexia.org/gordyiep.html

An HTML version of a booklet published by the Ohio Department of Education, it includes information on the IEP meeting, implementing the IEP, and reviewing the IEP.

Notes:

_____

_____

_____

_____

_____

Individualized Education Program: The Process

http://www.ldonline.org/ld_indepth/iep/iep_process.html

From the LD online site, this is a very good page describing all aspects of the IEP process from time lines to confidentiality.

Notes:

_____

_____

_____

_____

_____

Regulations Implementing IDEA

http://janWeb.icdi.wvu.edu/kinder/document.htm

This site features many documents that pertain to IDEA.

Notes:

_____

_____

_____

_____

_____

Regulations Implementing IDEA
(34 C.F.R. Part 300)

http://www.edlaw.net/public/iep_cont.htm

Full text of the Individuals with Disabilities Education Act includes a hyperlinked outline that lets you jump within sections.

Notes:

_____

_____

_____

_____

_____

Seven Habits of Highly Effective IEP Teams

http://www.ldonline.org/ld_indepth/iep/seven_habits.html

A short but informative page details the methods and strategies IEP team members should take to be a valuable member of the team.

Notes:

_____

_____

_____

_____

_____

Writing Individualized Education Programs for Success

http://www.ldonline.org/ld_indepth/iep/success_ieps.html

This is a very informative article by Dr. Barbara Bateman, a member of the Learning Disabilities Association.

Notes:

_____

_____

_____

_____

_____

Your Child's IEP—Practical and Legal Guidance for Parents
http://www.ldonline.org/ld_indepth/iep/iep_guidance.html

Along with tips and strategies for parents faced with their introduction into the world of IEPs, this site includes a good overview of the laws that pertain to IEPs and special education services (including recent court decisions).

Notes:

_____

_____

_____

_____

_____

_____

_____

_____

_____

_____

_____

_____

_____

_____

_____

Learning Disabilities

LD Online

http://www.ldonline.org/

This site is an interactive guide to learning disabilities for parents, teachers, and children. Categories: ABCs of LD/ADD, LD In Depth, LD Calendar, KidZone

Notes:

_____

_____

_____

_____

LD Resources

http://www.ldresources.com/

A very good site, it contains essays and articles about LD, links to other WWW sites devoted to LD, and much more. Categories: LD Reader, Articles and Essays, LD and Writing, LD Resources

Notes:

_____

_____

_____

_____

Learning Disabilities Center

http://www.coe.uga.edu/ldcenter/

From the University of Georgia comes a repository of online LD information. It contains contact information and Web sites (when available) to many special education organizations.

Notes:

_____

_____

_____

_____

National Center for Learning Disabilities

http://www.ncld.org/

The National Center for Learning Disabilities is a national not-for-profit organization committed to improving the lives of those affected by learning disabilities.

Notes:

_____

_____

_____

_____

Rebus Institute

http://www.cenatica.com/rebus/

This site is devoted to the dissemination of information related to adults with "learning differences."

Notes:

_____

_____

_____

_____

_____

_____

_____

_____

_____

_____

_____

_____

_____

_____

_____

_____

_____

_____

_____

_____

Physical Disabilities

American Association of People with Disabilities

http://www.aapd.com/

The AAPD strives to bring about "the next step in the evolution of the disability rights movement"—economic clout and power through numbers, unity, leadership, and impact.

Notes:

_____

_____

_____

_____

Curbcut.com

http://www.curbcut.com/

This is an excellent looking site designed for people confined to wheelchairs. Categories: Journals, People, Hope, Sex, Sports, Wheels, Travel, Home, Health, Women, Regional, Parenting, Law

Notes:

_____

_____

_____

_____

Denise's Toe Typed Home Page

http://www.sped.ukans.edu/~dlance/.index.html

This is the home page of Denise Lance, a doctoral student in Special Education at the University of Kansas. Her emphasis is in the application of technology in special education, including the use of assistive technology in literacy learning, helping students with physical and visual disabilities access the Internet, and the use of regular technology to train special educators.

Notes:

_____

_____

_____

_____

Disabled People's International

http://wpg-01.escape.ca/~dpi/

The purpose of DPI is to promote the Human Rights of People with Disabilities through full participation, equalization of opportunity, and development.

Notes:

_____

_____

_____

_____

Visual Impairment

Ability Home Page

http://www.ability.org/

This site is run by the UK charity Ability. Ability's objective is to "show that quality of life is related to how free a person is to make their own choices."

Notes:

_____

_____

_____

_____

American Council of the Blind

http://acb.org/

The American Council of the Blind (ACB) is the nation's leading membership organization of blind and visually impaired people. It was founded in 1961 and incorporated in the District of Columbia.

Notes:

_____

_____

_____

_____

Blindness Resource Center

http://www.nyise.org/blind.htm

This is a very extensive site with most everything you need from a site for the visually impaired on the Web. Categories: Access, Blindness, Braille History and Literacy, Deaf-Blind, Disabilities, Eye Conditions, Low Vision Resources, Online Info, Organizations, Research, Vendors, Links

Notes:

_____

_____

_____

_____

National Federation of the Blind

http://www.nfb.org/

The NFB's goal is the complete integration of the blind into society on a basis of equality. This site offers many resources for people with visual impairments.

Notes:

_____

_____

_____

_____

Technology

Computer as Learning Partner

http://www.clp.berkeley.edu/CLP.html

This is a description of a University at California, Berkley, research project where a wired classroom is used by eighth-graders as they are taught the physical science topics of heat, light, and sound.

Notes:

_____

_____

_____

_____

_____

Computer Teacher's Resource Page

http://nimbus.temple.edu/~jallis00/

This page contains links to Internet sites that can be used to create classroom projects for every subject in the elementary curriculum.

Notes:

_____

_____

_____

_____

_____

Computers 4 Kids

http://www.c4k.org/Pages/c4k.html

Computers 4 Kids accepts donated computers and selected technologies, refurbishes them, and then places them in schools through a grant review process.

Notes:

_____

_____

_____

_____

_____

Detwiler Foundation

http://www.detwiler.org/

A computers-for-school program, the Detwiler Foundation accepts donated computers and places them in classrooms.

Notes:

_____

_____

_____

_____

EdWeb: Exploring Technology and School Reform
http://edWeb.gsn.org/

With EdWeb, you can hunt down online educational resources around the world, learn about trends in education policy and information infrastructure development, examine success stories of computers in the classroom, and much, much more.

Notes:

_____

_____

_____

_____

Electronic Elementary Magazine: "The E-LINK"
http://www.inform.umd.edu/UMS+State/MDK12_Stuff/homepers/emag/

This magazine is a nonprofit, educational project that highlights interactive projects and creations of elementary grade students around the world.

Notes:

_____

_____

_____

_____

Electronic Learning

http://place.scholastic.com/el/index.htm

Lots of information about technology in the classroom, including new and archived articles, grant information, and a lot more can be found here.

Notes:

_____

_____

_____

_____

_____

Electronic School

http://www.electronic-school.com/

Published quarterly as a print and online supplement to *The American School Board Journal*, this is an excellent magazine site that provides full text articles and information for and about the wired school.

Notes:

_____

_____

_____

_____

_____

Global Schoolhouse

http://www.gsh.org/

Presented by the Global SchoolNet Foundation, this site features The Connected Educator, The Connected Classroom, and The Connected Learning Community.

Notes:

_____

_____

_____

_____

_____

Harnessing the Power of the Web: A Tutorial

http://www.gsn.org/Web/index.html

An unbelievably detailed lesson on how to integrate the Internet into the classroom and intended more for secondary education, this tutorial provides step-by-step instructions (and lessons) to using the Web for education.

Notes:

_____

_____

_____

_____

_____

Impact of Technology

http://www.mcrel.org/connect/tech/impact.html

This excellent resource features complete articles, surveys, etc., that explore the impact of technology in the classroom.

Notes:

_____

_____

_____

_____

_____

Internet Public Library

http://www.ipl.org/ipl/

This site features online lessons covering the Internet and other areas and contains a wide array of resources for students and teachers.

Notes:

_____

_____

_____

_____

_____

Learning on the Web 97

http://teleeducation.nb.ca/lotw/

Divided into 6 modules, this site from Canada takes the teacher from novice to expert in creating online education resources.

Notes:

_____

_____

_____

_____

_____

Netday National

http://www.netday96.com/

The Netday site describes the efforts to get every school in the U.S. wired for Internet access.

Notes:

_____

_____

_____

_____

_____

On the Horizon

http://sunsite.unc.edu/horizon/index.html

This site provides a meeting place for educators interested in technology issues. Also available are articles about educational technology research.

Notes:

_____

_____

_____

_____

_____

Road Map

http://Webreference.com/roadmap/

Roadmap96 is a free, 27-lesson Internet training workshop designed to teach new Net travelers how to travel around the rapidly expanding (and often confusing) "Information Superhighway" without getting lost. Very informative!

Notes:

_____

_____

_____

_____

_____

Tales from the Electronic Frontier

http://www.wested.org/tales/

This site presents the writings of ten teachers who share actual classroom experiences using the Internet in K–12 science and mathematics.

Notes:

_____

_____

_____

_____

_____

Technological Horizons in Education (T.H.E.)

http://www.thejournal.com/

Found here is news on the world of computers and related technologies, focusing on applications that improve teaching and learning for all ages. Categories: T.H.E. Forum, Events and Contests, Professional Development, Grants, Links

Notes:

_____

_____

_____

_____

_____

Technology and Learning Online

http://www.techlearning.com/

The online version of the magazine presents software reviews and articles on how to integrate technology into the curriculum.

Notes:

_____

_____

_____

_____

_____

Technology Connections

http://www.mcrel.org/connect/tech/index.html

From the Mid-continent Regional Educational Laboratory, this site offers articles on Internet safety, the impact of technology, and technology and teacher education.

Notes:

_____

_____

_____

_____

_____

Technology Counts—Key Reports

http://www.edweek.org/sreports/tc/intros/in-s2.htm

From the Education Week on the Web site comes a list of the "most informative recent reports on educational technology."

Notes:

_____

_____

_____

_____

Web 66-A K-12 World Wide Web Project

http://Web66.coled.umn.edu/

This highly-awarded site has 3 main goals: 1. To help K–12 educators learn how to set up their own Internet servers; 2. To link K–12 Web servers and the educators and students at those schools; 3. To help K–12 educators find and use K–12 appropriate resources on the Web—a very nice site!

Notes:

_____

_____

_____

_____

Web Developers Virtual Library

http://www.stars.com/

This is an indispensable site when you are trying to get that first home page up and running and an even better resource once you get hooked on HTML and want to start doing the fancy things.

Notes:

_____

_____

_____

_____

Writing HTML

http://www.mcli.dist.maricopa.edu/tut/

Learn to write your own home page by following this tutorial. The lessons are also available offline. It is written in a way so that anyone can understand the subtleties of HTML and designed to take teachers step-by-step through the process of creating Web pages.

Notes

_____

_____

_____

_____

Index

Index

Index

Index

For monthly updates to the urls in this book, visit our Web site at:

http://www.teachercreated.com/updates.html

---

http://www.teachercreated.com/updates.html

TCM
- Home
- What's New
- About Us
- Links

Our Products
- New Products
- TechWorks
- TechKNOWLEDGEy

Purchasing
- Find a Dealer Near You
- Order Online

Free Downloads
- Classroom Activities

Staff Development
- Seminars
- On Site Training

Request Information
- Contact Us

Feedback
- Guestbook **NEW!**
- Survey **Soon!**
- Submission Guidelines

Updated Links

This page contains updated links for Teacher Created Materials' Internet books. If you have found a dead link referred to in one of our books, you can report it here.

- TCM 2458--Internet Resources for Educators
- TCM 2460--Simple Internet Activities